How to Prepare For the CAT/6*

* CAT/ 6 is a registered trademark of Educational Testing Service, which was not involved in the production of and does not endorse this product

4th Grade Edition

By Lynn Jackson

carney
EDUCATIONAL SERVICES

CARNEY EDUCATIONAL SERVICES
Helping Students Help Themselves

1513 331356

Special thanks to Rim Namkoong, our illustrator

This book is dedicated to:

The moms and dads who get up early and stay up late. You are the true heroes, saving our future, one precious child at a time.

All the kids who don't make the evening news. To the wide-eyed children, full of love, energy, and wonder. You are as close to perfection as this world will ever see.

TABLE OF CONTENTS

An Overview of the CAT/6 Test

In the spring of 2002, the California Department of Education adopted the California Achievement Test, Sixth Edition (the CAT/6) as part of the state's Standardized Testing and Reporting System (STAR). The purpose behind this test is to provide California public school districts and parents with information about how their children are performing compared with other public school children from across the state. Keep in mind that this is a test of basic skills. It was written to assess the abilities of students only in specified areas of the curriculum. The CAT/6 is a standardized test, meaning that all public school children across California take the tests in the same manner and during the same months of the school year period. The directions given by teachers are the same, as are the amounts of time given to complete each testing section.

Why did California change from the SAT 9 to the CAT/6?

Over the last several years, the Stanford 9 (also referred to as SAT 9) standardized tests had generated controversy in some school districts due to errors in data analysis. Some of the important information reported by school districts was misused or analyzed incorrectly. These errors became quite costly to identify and correct. Additionally, some districts with large numbers of non-English speaking students encouraged parents to request waivers which would exclude their children from taking the SAT 9. Obviously, districts which sought to exclude such students from taking the test would receive higher scores than those districts which sought to test every student. In changing to the CAT/6, the California Board of Education decided to use a test with much more of a history in the state. The California Aptitude Tests were first developed in 1950, and are currently in use in nine other states. The CAT/6 will be administered by the Educational Testing Service (ETS), which is the largest testing firm in the nation.

What does the CAT/6 seek to measure?

Beginning in the spring of 2003, approximately 4.5 million students in grades 2-11 will be taking multiple choice tests in two main areas of the curriculum: Mathematics and Language Arts. The specific skills tested within Language Arts are vocabulary, reading comprehension, spelling, language mechanics (grammar), and language expression (word usage). The math sections of the test measure student mastery of math computation, math concepts and math applications. Students in grades 4-12 may be given a study skills subtest, which will measure how well student scan use information processing skills which they can use across all subject areas. The CAT test series also contains science and social studies subtests, but whether these will be used as part of the STAR program has yet to be determined.

Why do schools give standardized tests?

The CAT/6 gives schools an idea of how well they are teaching basic skills which all students need to be successful in the future. These skills are defined for schools in documents called "State Standards." The State Department of Education has spelled out for teachers, parents and students what they should be learning in each academic subject during a given school year. Schools receive data about how their students performed both individually and by grade level. Which state standards did students meet? Which standards need to be taught differently next year? How can schools help each child move toward meeting all the standards? All of these questions can be best answered by using the data provided by the CAT/6. Standardized tests are valuable because they are an objective way to measure how successfully schools are delivering the basics. The idea behind standardizing the test is this: if every public school student takes the same tests in the same way, then it is a fair way to compare schools and districts. If, for example, one school gave children an extra 5 hours to complete the test, then it would be an unfair advantage given to those children.

What about criticism of standardized tests?

In the last few years, criticism of standardized tests has mounted. Many parents and teachers say that preparing for these tests takes away time from valuable subjects like art, drama and music. They have also noted the stressful nature of these tests and question whether it is healthy to subject young children to this type of pressure to perform. Others believe these tests reward wealthy school districts in the suburbs, while they punish inner-city school districts with large numbers of non-English speaking students. While some of these criticisms are valid, they do not change the fact that standardized tests are widely regarded as the best way for schools to measure how they are teaching to the California State Standards. As long as the public asks public schools to prove they are doing an effective job educating children, these tests will be with us. The criticism of the Stanford 9 test resulted in replacing it with the CAT/6, which is ANOTHER standardized test.

As parents, we need to realize that these tests have become a fact of life in California public schools and help children prepare for them. Certainly, schools and teachers are primarily responsible for preparing your child for these tests. Yet parents have an important role to play. This book will give you many valuable tools you can use in helping your child do their best on this very important standardized test. It is the job of California public schools to teach to the standards, which are tested on the CAT/6, but your role as a reinforcer of skills and a supporter of your child's progress as a student cannot be ignored.

How Your Child Can Improve His/Her Score On ANY Multiple Choice Standardized Test

Your child has entered an educational world that is run by standardized tests. Students take the Scholastic Aptitude Test (SAT) to help them get into college and the Graduate Record Examination (GRE) to help them get into graduate school. Other exams like the ACT and the PSAT are not as well-known, but also very important to your child's future success. Schools spend a great deal of time teaching children the material they need to know to do well on these tests, but very little time teaching children HOW to take these tests. This is a gap that parents can easily fill. To begin with, you can look for opportunities to strengthen your child's reading and vocabulary skills as well as his/her ability to follow detailed written directions.

The importance of reading:

Students who do well on standardized tests tend to be excellent readers. They read frequently for pleasure and have a good understanding of what they have read. You can help support your child as a reader by helping him/her set aside a regular time to read each and every day. As you may know, children tend to be successful when they follow an established pattern of behavior. Even 15-20 minutes spent reading a magazine or newspaper before bedtime will help. Children should read both fiction and non-fiction material at home, as well as at school. Ask your child about what s/he has read. Help him/her to make connections between a book s/he is currently reading and a movie or a television show s/he has recently seen. THE BOTTOM LINE: Children who read well will do better on the test than children who do not. There is written material in all sections of the test that must be quickly comprehended. Even the math sections have written information contained in each question.

The importance of building a larger vocabulary:

As you may know, children who read well and who read often tend to have a large vocabulary. This is important since there is an entire section of the test that is devoted exclusively to the use of vocabulary words. You can support your child in attempting to improve his/her vocabulary by encouraging him/her to read challenging material on a regular basis. The newspaper is a good place to start. Studies have shown that many newspaper articles are written on a 4th to 5th grade reading level! Help your child to use new and more difficult words both in his/her own conversations and in his/her writings. If you use an advanced vocabulary when speaking to your children, don't be surprised if they begin to incorporate some of the new words into his/her daily speech. One of the most immediate ways to judge the intelligence of anyone is in his/her use of language. Children are aware of this too. THE BOTTOM LINE: Children who have an expansive vocabulary will do better on the test than children who do not. Find as many ways as possible to help build new words into your child's speech and writing.

The importance of following written directions:

The test is a teacher-directed test. Teachers tell students how to complete each section of the test and give them specific examples that are designed to help them understand what to do. However, teachers are not allowed to help students once each test has begun. The written script for teachers seems to repeat one phrase continually: "READ THE DIRECTIONS CAREFULLY." This is certainly not an accident. Students face a series of questions that cannot be answered correctly unless they clearly understand what is being asked. Help your child by giving him/her a series of tasks to complete at home in writing. Directions should be multi-step and should be as detailed as possible without frustrating your child. For example: "Please take out the trash cans this afternoon. Place all the bottles and cans in the blue recycling bin and place all the extra newspapers that are stacked in the garage in the yellow recycling bin." If children are able to follow these types of directions and are able to reread to clarify what is being asked, they will be at a tremendous advantage when it comes to the test.
THE BOTTOM LINE: Children who are able to follow a series of detailed, written directions will have a tremendous advantage over those who are unable to do so.

All of the previous suggestions are designed to be used before the test is actually given to help your child improve in some basic test-taking skills. Here are some strategies that you can teach your child to use once s/he is taking the test:

1. **SELECT THE BEST ANSWER.**

The test, like many multiple-choice tests, isn't designed for children to write their own answers to the questions. They will fill in a bubble by the four answer choices and select the BEST possible answer. Reading the question carefully is quite important, since the question may contain key words needed to select the correct answer. For example:

The first President of the United States was

a. John Adams.
b. James Madison.
c. George Washington.
d. Thomas Jefferson.

The correct answer is, of course, "c". Students would need to read the question carefully and focus on the key word in the question: "first". All of the names listed were Presidents of the United States early in our history, but only choice "c" contains the name of our first President. Looking for key words like "least" or "greater" will help your child to select the best answer from among the choices given.

2. ANSWER THE EASY QUESTIONS FIRST.

The test contains a series of timed tests. Children who waste time on a difficult question found at the beginning of a test may run out of time before they finish the entire test. A good strategy is to skip anything that seems too difficult to answer immediately. Once your children have answered every "easy" question in the section, they can go back through the test and spend more time working on the more time-consuming questions. If students are given only 30 minutes to answer 25 reading vocabulary questions, they shouldn't spend much more than a minute on each one. Wasting four or five minutes on one question is not a good idea, since it reduces the amount of time your child will have to work on the rest of the test. Once time runs out, that's it! Any questions left unanswered will be counted wrong when the test is machine scored. Working on the easier questions first will allow your child to make the best use of the allowed time.

3. ELIMINATE ANY UNREASONABLE ANSWER CHOICES.

No matter how intelligent your child is, it is inevitable that s/he will come to a test question that s/he finds too difficult to answer. In this situation, the best thing to do is to make an "educated guess." If students can eliminate one or more of the answer choices given, they have a much greater chance of answering the question correctly.

For example:

Select the word below that means the same as the underlined word:

Jennifer became <u>enraged</u> when she found out her diary had been read.

  a. mournful
  b. furious
  c. pleased
  d. depressed

Even if your child didn't know that "b" is the best answer choice, s/he could certainly eliminate choice "c" from consideration. Clearly, Jennifer would not be "pleased" to find out her diary had been read.

4. DO MATH QUESTIONS ON PAPER WHEN NECESSARY.

The math sections of the test cause children problems because several of the answer choices seem like they could be correct. The only way to select the best answer choice for some math questions is to do the math calculation on scratch paper. The answer choices given for these questions are written to discourage guessing.

For example:

Eileen has saved $3245 to buy a car. Her aunt gave her another $250 as a gift. How much does she have in all?

    a. $3595
    b. $4495
    c. $3495
    d. $3485

The correct answer is "c", but it is hard to select the correct answer because all of the answer choices seem similar. The best way to determine the correct answer would be to add $3245 and $250 on scratch paper.

> If you work with your children with these simple strategies, you will find that they will approach these tests with confidence, rather than with anxiety. Teach your children to prepare and then to approach the test with a positive attitude. They should be able to say to themselves, "I know this stuff, I'll do a great job today."

LANGUAGE ARTS

Content Cluster: SYNONYMS

Objective: *To evaluate knowledge of word choice and meaning.*

Parent Tip: To help your child expand her vocabulary, be sure to read with your child on a regular basis and discuss new and challenging vocabulary as it comes up. Offer a simpler, more common word meaning for sophisticated vocabulary. Consider having your child maintain a vocabulary journal or word box with new words and their meanings. To develop and expand vocabulary skills, it is important to have your child do some supported reading at a challenging level. Reading aloud or reading together is best for this.

Select a synonym to match the <u>underlined</u> word.

Example: A <u>wood</u> pile.

   a. scrap
   b. lumber
   c. plywood
   d. log

The correct answer is "b". Lumber is the synonym for wood.

Practice Questions:

1. To <u>buy</u> goods

   a. sell
   b. bring
   c. purchase
   d. send

2. <u>Mix</u> carefully

   a. combine
   b. separate
   c. join
   d. enter

3. A <u>victorious</u> team

   a. victory
   b. creative
   c. hard working
   d. triumphant

4. To <u>fly</u> is to

   a. cast
   b. soar
   c. dive
   d. shun

5. Good <u>luck</u>

   a. bye
   b. time
   c. fortune
   d. money

6. A large <u>country</u>

   a. state
   b. city
   c. district
   d. nation

7. Once in a lifetime <u>chance</u>

   a. opportunity
   b. experience
   c. character
   d. performance

8. <u>Choose</u> a book

   a. read
   b. buy
   c. select
   d. edit

9. careless <u>mistake</u>

   a. notion
   b. error
   c. blunder
   d. eruption

10. To <u>brag</u> about oneself is to

   a. tattle
   b. persevere
   c. bubble
   d. boast

11. The hero was <u>brave</u>

   a. brash
   b. courageous
   c. weak
   d. strong

12. He was a <u>humble</u> man

   a. modest
   b. modern
   c. pleasant
   d. wealthy

13. To <u>shake</u> is to

   a. rattle
   b. roll
   c. wander
   d. quiver

14. <u>Push</u> <u>gently</u>

   a. pull
   b. shove
   c. yank
   d. nudge

Content Cluster: ANTONYMS

Objective: To evaluate knowledge of word choice and meaning

Parent Tip: To help your child expand his vocabulary, be sure to read with your child on a regular basis and discuss new and challenging vocabulary as it comes up. Offer a simpler, more common word meaning for sophisticated vocabulary. Compare words with their *opposite* meanings. Consider having your child maintain a vocabulary journal or word box with new words and their meanings. To develop and expand vocabulary skills, it is important to have your child do some supported reading at a challenging level. Reading aloud or reading together is best for this.

Select an antonym to match the <u>underlined</u> world.

Example: That puppy is <u>plump</u>.

     a. fat
     b. round
     c. odd
     d. slender

The correct answer is "d". Slender is an antonym for the word plump.

Practice Question:

1. The puzzle pieces can <u>connect</u>.

     a. combine
     b. join
     c. separate
     d. splinter

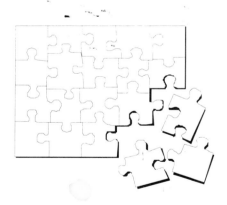

2. Do not <u>expose</u> the answer.

     a. show
     b. tell
     c. freeze
     d. conceal

3. Be sure to send the <u>original</u>.

   a. certificate
   b. copy
   c. document
   d. authentic

4. Mr. Smith will <u>repair</u> the model.

   a. fix
   b. adjust
   c. maintain
   d. wreck

5. Sam can be very <u>sloppy</u>.

   a. messy
   b. dirty
   c. clean
   d. meticulous

6. The cookies were <u>different</u>.

   a. similar
   b. tasty
   c. unusual
   d. unique

7. The policeman said to <u>stop</u>.

   a. wait
   b. hold
   c. proceed
   d. panic

8. The <u>amateur</u> athlete entered the tournament.

   a. professional
   b. inexperienced
   c. experienced
   d. childish

9. The <u>expensive</u> gift was lost.

    a. costly
    b. inexpensive
    c. pricey
    d. priceless

10. The rain began to <u>dwindle</u>.

    a. stop
    b. halt
    c. increase
    d. pour

11. Please <u>confirm</u> your answer.

    a. reply
    b. address
    c. state
    d. deny

12. There was the <u>presence</u> of a skunk in the area.

    a. location
    b. absence
    c. viability
    d. critter

13. The day was very <u>cheerful</u>.

    a. happy
    b. bright
    c. gay
    d. glum

14. They used <u>artificial</u> flowers.

    a. genuine
    b. fake
    c. odd
    d. old

Content Cluster: CONTEXT

Objective: To evaluate knowledge of word choice and meaning

Parent Tip: Help your children to read the selection thoroughly BEFORE choosing the best word for the answer. Many students will make errors because they are not aware of the complete meaning of the selection and stop at the blank to choose a word.

Choose the best answer.

Read the selection and then find the words below to complete the paragraph.

The children had decided it was time to 1. _____ a new tree house. New lumber was
2. _____ as the old wood had become 3. _____ by termites. First, the children
4. _____ the old tree house, trying to 5. _____ reusable nails. Next, they
designed an 6. _____ plan to rebuild. Then, they began the 7. _____ of cutting
and 8. _____ the boards in place. Before they knew it, the tree house was 9. _____
and ready for 10. _____.

---

1. a. forfeit
    b. balance
    c. erect
    d. destroy

2. a. essential
    b. unnecessary
    c. silly
    d. certain

3. a. stronger
    b. stung
    c. damaged
    d. endangered

4. a. rebuilt
    b. reconnected
    c. joined
    d. disassembled

5.　a.　recycle
　　b.　rekindle
　　c.　reuse
　　d.　remake

6.　a.　lesson
　　b.　team
　　c.　architectural
　　d.　television

7.　a.　method
　　b.　process
　　c.　problem
　　d.　troubleshoot

8.　a.　stamping
　　b.　joining
　　c.　handling
　　d.　nailing

9.　a.　complete
　　b.　organized
　　c.　concluded
　　d.　obsolete

10.　a.　termites
　　b.　television
　　c.　occupation
　　d.　turmoil

Content Cluster: MULTIPLE MEANINGS

Objective: To evaluate word choice in multiple meaning situations.

Parent Tip: Help your child to understand that many words in the English language have more than one meaning. It is important to know how to use the words appropriately. For example, the word "case" can refer to a case of soda, a case of measles, a legal case, or a briefcase. Expanding vocabulary in general, will help your child become more aware of multiple meanings for words.

Choose the best answer that fits both sentences.

Example:

The sun cast a bright _____.
The canoe was very _____.

       a. shine
       b. ray
       c. light
       d. tight

The correct answer is "c". Light fits both sentences.

Practice Questions:

1. The car needs a _____ up.
   She can sing a sweet _____.

       a. blow
       b. song
       c. melody
       d. tune

2. Paint will _____ up the house.
   The tree was a blue _____.

       a. brighten
       b. clean
       c. pine
       d. spruce

3. The automobile _____ closes at 4:30.
   Did you _____ the roses?

   a. factory
   b. buy
   c. adjust
   d. plant

4. The table _____ decorated the dining room table.
   Mr. Smyth sent a _____ with a message.

   a. topper
   b. student
   c. runner
   d. decorator

5. Cake _____ can be messy!
   Who is the next _____ in the line-up?

   a. hitter
   b. batter
   c. mix
   d. player

6. Be careful not to _____ the truck into the wall.
   The young _____ climbed the rocks well.

   a. pluck
   b. chick
   c. ram
   d. hooves

7. The _____ did not stick to the wall.
   We needed a _____ to record the movie.

   a. glue
   b. paper
   c. tape
   d. pin

Content Cluster: SENTENCE STRUCTURE AND USAGE

Objective: To evaluate knowledge of correct sentence structure and word usage such as noun-verb agreement.

Parent Tip: To help your children to make correct choices in noun-verb agreement when writing and speaking, reinforce correct grammar skills and correct grammatical errors when they occur.

Choose the best answer:

Example: Tim and _____ will be there.

        a. me
        b. I
        c. you
        d. them

The correct answer is "b". I is the best answer to the sentence.

Practice Questions:

1. Many children _____ coming to the party tomorrow.

        a. will
        b. have been
        c. are
        d. will not

2. Will _____ need help today?

        a. me
        b. you
        c. us
        d. that

3. It is _____ toy.

    a. there
    b. their
    c. them
    d. those

4. _____ you going to join us?

    a. Will
    b. Won't
    c. Were
    d. We're

Choose the correct complete sentence.

5. a. The field trip was a good learning experience.
    b. The field trip were a well learning experience.
    c. The field trip weren't a good learning experience.
    d. None are correct.

6. a. Jimmy did good on his test.
    b. Jimmy didn't do good on his test.
    c. Jimmy did well on his test.
    d. None are correct.

7. a. Fables is a favorite one of mine.
    b. Fables are favorites of mine.
    c. Fables are favorite of mine.
    d. None are correct.

8. a. The painters finished his work early.
    b. The painters finished early.
    c. The painters finished there work early.
    d. None are correct.

9. a. Traveling quickly, the thieves got away.
    b. Traveling more quick, the thieves got a way.
    c. Traveling quick, the thieves got away.
    d. None are correct.

Content Cluster: FIGURATIVE LANGUAGE SKILLS

Objective: To evaluate knowledge of figurative language writing techniques such as simile, metaphor, hyperbole, and personification.

> **Parent Tip:** Help your children to recognize these writing techniques that enhance writing. They should be familiar with the difference between simile and metaphor. A metaphor is a comparison between two things that are not alike. If a comparison uses the word "like" or the word "as", then it is called a simile. Hyperbole is the use of exaggeration, and personification is the giving of human characteristics to non-living objects.

Example:

Metaphor:	Math is a blizzard of symbols.
Simile:	Life is like a box of candy.
Hyperbole:	We had to wait an eternity to see the doctor.
Personification:	The whining teakettle called to us.

Figurative language is defined as the use of a word or phrase to mean something quite different from its literal or general meaning. The statement, "I can see right through you," means something quite different than actually being able to see through a person.

Choose the best category for each statement.

1. An army of ants marched across the picnic table.

    a. metaphor
    b. simile
    c. hyperbole
    d. personification

2. The spaghetti slithered off my fork.

    a. metaphor
    b. simile
    c. hyperbole
    d. personification

3. The child was as cool as a cucumber.

    a. metaphor
    b. simile
    c. hyperbole
    d. personification

4. My temper is as hot as a branding iron.

    a. metaphor
    b. simile
    c. hyperbole
    d. personification

5. The race was over in a flash.

    a. metaphor
    b. simile
    c. hyperbole
    d. personification

6. The computer tormented me by flashing unknown statements.

    a. metaphor
    b. simile
    c. hyperbole
    d. personification

7. The cake tasted like rivers of fudge.

    a. metaphor
    b. simile
    c. hyperbole
    d. personification

8. We waited forever for Steven to call.

    a. metaphor
    b. simile
    c. hyperbole
    d. personification

9. The sunset was like a giant pumpkin.

   a. metaphor
   b. simile
   c. hyperbole
   d. personification

10. Tom Smith is a gem of a guy.

    a. metaphor
    b. simile
    c. hyperbole
    d. personification

11. The play lasted a lifetime.

    a. metaphor
    b. simile
    c. hyperbole
    d. personification

12. The coughing engine broke down.

    a. metaphor
    b. simile
    c. hyperbole
    d. personification

13. Powdered sugar is light as snow.

    a. metaphor
    b. simile
    c. hyperbole
    d. personification

14. The thunderclouds looked as gray as steel.

    a. metaphor
    b. simile
    c. hyperbole
    d. personification

Content Cluster: CAPITALIZATION AND PUNCTUATION

Objective: To evaluate knowledge of correct mechanics of writing.

> **Parent Tip:** Help your children learn about correct capitalization and punctuation by reinforcing rules as you read all types of materials with your child. Take note of punctuation in newspapers, stories, business letters, and textbooks, and point them out.

Choose the best answer.

Example:

Mrs. Smith and steven went to a museum.
- a. Mrs Smith and steven
- b. Mrs. Smith and Steven
- c. Mrs. Smith. and Steven
- d. No mistakes

The correct answer is "b". Mrs. Smith and Steven is the best answer.

Practice Questions:

1. The jackson twins are coming to the party.

   a. the jackson twins are coming to the party?
   b. The jackson twins are coming to the party?
   c. The Jackson twins are coming to the party.
   d. No mistakes

2. How will you get to New york

   a. How will you get to New York.
   b. How will you get to New York?
   c. How will you get to New York!
   d. No mistakes

3. Please select blueberries cherries, and plums at the store

   a. Please select blueberries, cherries and plums, at the store.
   b. Please select blueberries, cherries, and plums, at the store.
   c. Please select blueberries, cherries, and plums at the store.
   d. No mistakes.

4. On Thursday, May 5, 1999 school will be closed.
    a. On Thursday May 5, 1999, school will be closed.
    b. On Thursday, May, 5, 1999 school will be closed.
    c. On Thursday, May 5, 1999, school will be closed.
    d. No mistakes

5. The four seasons are spring summer autumn, and winter.

    a. The four seasons are spring summer, autumn and winter.
    b. The four seasons are spring, summer, autumn, and winter.
    c. The four seasons are spring, summer, autumn and winter.
    d. No mistakes

6. You should read a book called By the Great Horn Spoon

    a. You should read a book called "By the Great Horn Spoon"
    b. You should read a book called <u>By the Great Horn Spoon</u>.
    c. You should read a book called By the great horn spoon.
    d. No mistakes

7. Jacob asked "What time is it?

    a. Jacob, asked "What time is it"?
    b. Jacob asked, "What time is it?"
    c. Jacob asked, What time is it?
    d. No mistakes

8. Creative art is the best exclaimed Anne

    a. Creative art is the best exclaimed Anne!
    b. Creative art is the best, exclaimed Anne!
    c. "Creative art is the best!" exclaimed Anne.
    d. No mistakes

9. We saw students paintings in The Kids Book of Art.

    a. We saw students' paintings in <u>The Kids Book of Art</u>.
    b. We saw students' paintings in <u>The Kid's Book of Art</u>.
    c. We saw student's paintings in The kid's Book of Art.
    d. No mistakes

Content Cluster: READING COMPREHENSION

Objective: To evaluate reading skills using different types of materials.

> **Parent Tip:** To help your child with reading strategies for test taking, have her read the associated questions first. This helps to set some background and focus for the sample she will be reading. Then, she should read the entire selection thoroughly. As she attempts to answer follow up questions, she should go back into the selection and locate supporting statements to verify her choice of answer.

Read the selection and answer the questions that follow:

Stacy was ecstatic. She had been waiting for three weeks for this special Saturday to arrive. Today, Stacy and her family are driving into the country to select their new Siberian Husky puppy. The entire family is excited about this new arrival.

As they drive to the kennel, Stacy and her sister, Corinne, begin selecting possible new names. They try out such titles as Fuzzball, King, Champ, Queenie, and Scout. The girls' parents encourage them to wait until they choose their new puppy. They don't know if they will choose a boy or a girl. They are also reminded that the puppy's personality may trigger the ideal name.

At the kennel, everyone is led to a grassy pasture that is fenced off. In the far corner, there appears to be a mass of fur. As they approach, everyone notices simultaneously that the mass of fur is really a pile of sleeping puppies. Not three, not six, but twelve adorable puppies! How would Stacy know which one to pick? As they roused the puppies, they eagerly sprang to life. Licking, tripping, frolicking puppies were everywhere. Everyone was giggling as the puppies vied for attention. However, there were two little ones that stayed off to the side and appeared somewhat shy. Stacy strolled over to those two and sat down beside them. Before she knew it they had crawled into her lap and started licking her hand. Stacy quickly realized she had a big problem.

On the drive home, everyone participated in suggesting names for the adorable pair of furry bookends. Bert and Ernie, Tweety and Sylvester, or Pooh and Tigger were ideas that came to mind, but in the end, Stacy liked the simplicity of Jack and Jill.

1. Which sentence from the first passage best states the main idea of the selection?

    a. Stacy was ecstatic.
    b. She had been waiting for three weeks for this special Saturday to arrive.
    c. Today, Stacy and her family are driving into the country to select their new Siberian Husky puppy.
    d. The entire family is excited about this new arrival.

2. The word "trigger" most closely means:

    a. a part of a gun
    b. to trip
    c. to make aware
    d. to calm

3. On what day will Stacy get her puppy?

    a. Sunday
    b. Saturday
    c. Friday
    d. Thursday

4. Why do the parents encourage the girls to wait to name the puppy?

    a. Puppies should not be named in advance.
    b. The puppies already had names.
    c. Using the puppy's personality might help to select a name.
    d. They will pick a name from a list.

5. How many puppies were there to choose from?

    a. 2
    b. 3
    c. 6
    d. 12

6. The term "roused" means:

    a. agitated
    b. awakened
    c. irritated
    d. selected

7. The phrase "vied for attention" means:

    a. begged
    b. tries to be noticed
    c. calls for help
    d. cries out

8. What was Stacy's "big problem?"

   a. She didn't know which of the twelve puppies to select.
   b. She didn't know which of the two puppies to select.
   c. She didn't want to select any of the puppies.
   d. She didn't know how to pick a puppy.

9. Which conclusion can you draw from the end of the story?

   a. Everyone in Stacy's family likes puppies.
   b. Stacy was able to select two puppies instead of one.
   c. The puppies were going to a good home.
   d. The puppies will be happier at Stacy's than at the kennel.

   For the first ten years of his life, Cesar Chavez lived on a small farm near Yuma, Arizona. He and his family were Mexican Americans who spoke Spanish. They lived with other Mexican Americans who were very poor and grew the food they ate on land they had owned. These families were unable to pay taxes, and the government took their land away. Many of these families became migrant workers and moved to California. Migrant workers travel from farm to farm picking crops as they are ready to be harvested.

   Cesar Chavez and his family moved to California when he was ten years old. Life was hard. The migrant families lived in sub-standard housing with no running water. Their employers were English-speaking farm owners who weren't very interested in the problems of the migrant families. Schooling was difficult for children of migrant workers. Many children worked in the fields and never went to school. Others went to school sporadically. Cesar had gone to 30 different schools by the time he entered the eighth grade. Cesar was a determined student and did learn to speak and read English.

   As an adult, Cesar became a leader of migrant workers and fought for their rights. He encouraged them, and helped them to learn to read and to vote. He formed the National Farm Worker's Association, a union to protect the rights of farm workers. He is well known for leading strikes, such as the grape workers strike of 1965. This strike was organized to be sure that the farm owners recognized the migrants' right to unite.

10. This selection is about:

    a. migrant workers
    b. Cesar Chavez
    c. migrant schools
    d. union rights

11. For what reason did the Mexican Americans lose their land to the government?

   a. They were unable to grow enough food.
   b. The government said that Mexican Americans could not own land.
   c. The Mexican Americans were unable to pay taxes.
   d. The Mexican Americans wanted to give their land away.

12. The term "migrant" means:

   a. moving from place to place
   b. living in poor conditions
   c. fruit and vegetable picker
   d. farmer

13. The sentence, "Life was hard," refers to:

   a. living in hard, rocky areas
   b. being hardheaded
   c. living in a difficult situation
   d. hard work

14. Why do you think the English-speaking farm owners were not interested in the problems of the migrant families?

   a. The farm owners were lazy.
   b. The farm owners didn't want to take the time and spend the money to improve things.
   c. The farm owners were poor and couldn't help the migrant families.
   d. The farm owners didn't like the migrant families.

15. Schooling was difficult for migrant children because

   a. their parents didn't speak English and couldn't help them.
   b. migrant children moved around frequently and often missed school.
   c. the teachers didn't want to teach migrant children.
   d. they were frequently sick and missed school.

16. The term "sporadically" means:

   a. frequently
   b. infrequently
   c. often
   d. never

17. A <u>union</u> is most likely

    a. two or more workers working together.
    b. a system of farm owners.
    c. an organization that fights for fair work practices.
    d. a factory.

18. What do you learn about Cesar Chavez's personality in reading this selection?

    a. He was a poor child.
    b. He was a migrant worker.
    c. He learned to read English.
    d. He cared about how he and others were treated.

19. The main idea of this section is:

    a. Migrant workers are often poor.
    b. Cesar Chavez became a leader for migrant workers.
    c. Cesar Chavez often fought people to get attention.
    d. Migrant workers are important to farming.

There are about seventy-five different kinds of whales. The blue whale is not only the biggest whale, but also the biggest animal in the world. The smallest of all whales is called a pygmy sperm whale. The sperm whale is identified by its over-sized head. A narwhal is a type of whale that has a tooth that grows from its head. It can grow to be as long as ten feet!

Whales are the largest creatures that roam our oceans. They are categorized as mammals and give birth to a baby whale called a calf. As with other mammals, the calf drinks its mother's milk until it can feed itself.

Whales breathe through a special hole called a blowhole. Water shoots out of the blowhole as the whale surfaces. When a whale is underwater, it is actually holding its breath. This is one example of how whales are not fish. A second example is that when whales are sleepy, they will lie on top of the water and take a nap!

Whales make unusual sounds that they use to communicate with each other. They seem to almost be singing. Humpback whales are well known for the unique sounds they make. Scientists are very interested in studying the sounds of the humpback and learning more about their methods of communication.

Whales are often called gentle giants, but a certain whale is known as the killer whale. Orcas hunt seals, large fish, and even other whales. They are the black and white whales that you will find at Sea World. Shamu is an Orca whale that has been trained to do tricks. As you may have guessed, Orcas are very smart.

Many whales have become endangered species. They had been hunted for their blubber that was used as an energy source. Today, there are laws to protect whales that have helped them increase in number. Whales are interesting creatures that give character to our oceans.

20. The blue whale is

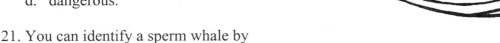

   a. blue.
   b. the largest whale.
   c. a type of narwhal.
   d. dangerous.

21. You can identify a sperm whale by

   a. looking for its horn like tooth.
   b. looking for stripes and spots on its skin.
   c. looking for its oversized head.
   d. looking for a hammer shaped head.

22. Which of the following characteristics do only mammals have in common?

   a. They all have skin.
   b. They nurse their young with mother's milk.
   c. They breathe underwater.
   d. They eat meat.

23. A baby whale is called a

   a. cub.
   b. pup.
   c. pony.
   d. calf.

24. What purpose does a "blowhole" serve?

   a. It allows the whale to breathe.
   b. It helps the whale to float.
   c. It gives out unusual sounds.
   d. It is a play tool.

25. How do whales rest when they are tired?

   a. They sleep at the bottom of the ocean or along a reef.
   b. They sleep in a shallow cove.
   c. They do not rest at all.
   d. They float atop the water's surface.

26. The term "communicate" means

    a. to share.
    b. to talk.
    c. to eat.
    d. to find.

27. The term "methods" means

    a. a process
    b. a system
    c. a procedure for
    d. all of the above

28. Gentle Giant may not be the best nickname for whales because

    a. they are always gentle and kind.
    b. whales are very shy.
    c. some whales are known to be killer whales.
    d. whales are very smart.

29. <u>Blubber</u> most likely is

    a. whale teeth.
    b. whale tail.
    c. whale fat.
    d. barnacles.

30. Which sentence best summarizes the selection?

    a. Whales are gentle giants.
    b. Whales are mammals.
    c. Whales are interesting creatures that roam our oceans.
    d. There are seventy-five different kinds of whales.

While reading <u>Over the Top of the World,</u> by Will Steger and Jon Bowermaster, I was struck by a section about pollution in the Arctic. Will Steger is well known for his dogsled adventure across the Arctic Ocean. They traveled by dogsled and canoe sled during a four-month trek that crossed the ice-covered terrain formed by the frozen Arctic Ocean. The book explores all aspects of their expedition, as well as intriguing facts about Arctic life.

The section on pollution caught my eye, as I had a hard time associating pollution with a frozen ocean mass. But unfortunately, not even the Arctic Ocean is able to avoid the destructive effects of pollutants. It begins by discussing the patterns of ocean currents, and how they travel from the mid-latitudes to the Arctic region and back down again. In these currents, scientists have discovered evidence of pesticides that come from cities and farms. "In a process known as 'transboundary pollution,' these contaminants enter the atmosphere or a river system and are carried to the Arctic." Amazingly, or perhaps not so amazingly, these pesticides are not easily dissipated. The cold climate acts as a preserving agent. The book cites an example of a chemical that has a warm climate life of 8 months, and an Arctic life of possibly 40 years.

The greatest concern is that these pesticides enter the food web where they threaten the local species. These "contaminants" are found in fish. Seals eat the fish. Polar bears and the local Inuit people then eat seals. The long-term effects of these pollutants are still to be seen, but they can only be negative. It's frightening to realize that the source of these poisons is "thousands of miles away in areas such as India, Europe, and the United States."

31. The term "struck" most closely means:

    a. hit on the head
    b. caught the attention of
    c. hit a wall
    d. hand on a clock at midnight

32. Which sentence from the selection best states the main idea?

    a. The section on pollution caught my eye, as I had a hard time associating pollution with a frozen ocean mass.
    b. But unfortunately, not even the Arctic Ocean is able to avoid the destructive effects of pollutants.
    c. It begins by discussing the patterns of ocean currents, and how they travel from the mid-latitudes to the Arctic region and back down again.
    d. In these currents, scientists have discovered evidence of pesticides that come from cities and farms.

33. The term "terrain" refers to

   a. land surface
   b. water
   c. currents
   d. pollution

34. The term "mid-latitudes" is referring to

   a. areas near the poles.
   b. areas near the prime meridian.
   c. the Arctic region.
   d. areas north and south of the equator.

35. Pesticides are also

   a. toxins
   b. poisons
   c. pollutants
   d. all of the above

36. "Transboundary Pollution" can best be explained as

   a. the movement of pollutants from one area to another.
   b. pollution problems related to recycling plastics.
   c. pollution in boundary zones.
   d. illegal dumping.

37. The term "dissipated" means

   a. to build up
   b. to break down
   c. to regroup
   d. to reorganize

38. What effect does cold have on pesticides?

   a. It reduces their life span.
   b. It reduces their cost.
   c. It increases their life span.
   d. It increases their cost.

39. Which statement best explains how the pesticides got into the river system in the beginning?

    a. Companies dumped pesticides directly into rivers.
    b. Rain created a run-off effect that carried pesticides from farmland and cities to local waterways.
    c. Pesticides are eaten by river wildlife.
    d. Pesticides evaporate into the air and become toxic clouds.

40. What role does the food web play in this problem?

    a. It demonstrates the long-term effects of pollution.
    b. It demonstrates what animals live in the arctic region.
    c. It helps scientists to know which animals live where and eat what.
    d. It shows a chain of producers and consumers and their role in an ecosystem.

41. What is likely to happen if transboundary pollution continues?

    a. The ozone layer will get thicker.
    b. Scientists will go and study Antarctica.
    c. Pollution will increase and animals will be endangered.
    d. The polar regions will have an increase in animal species.

42. Which solution listed below is most logical for this selection?

    a. Change ocean currents so that pollution is not carried to the Arctic region.
    b. The Inuit people should not eat the fish and seal.
    c. Scientists should continue to study the Arctic region.
    d. Improved pollution controls should be put into effect in Europe, Asia, and the United States.

Bryan had volunteered to bake some cookies for the school fund-raiser. The students were trying to raise funds for a class trip to the Metropolitan Museum of Art in New York City. Each student was required to participate in at least one fund-raiser. There was a bake sale, a car wash, pizza sales, and a "students for hire" program. Bryan chose the bake sale and the "students for hire" program.

When Bryan got home after school, he started to make the cookies. He had decided he would make oatmeal-chocolate chip cookies. He had never made them before because his mom was usually the baker in the family. Bryan figured he could read the directions and it would all fall into place. What Bryan didn't plan for was that his mother's recipe card had several stains on it that had blotted out some of the ingredients and the directions. Luckily, he could figure out the ingredients, but the directions were sketchy.

Bryan wrote down what he could read on a separate piece of paper. He wrote:

Work in flour and baking soda to wet mixture.
Last, stir in oats, chocolate chips, and nuts. Mix well.
Next, add eggs, milk, and vanilla. Beat thoroughly.
First, heat oven to 375 degrees F.
Begin by beating butter and sugar until creamy.
Drop dough onto cookie sheet and bake for 9-10 minutes.

Now he had to figure out the correct order. Bryan used his common sense and ended up with 4 dozen tasty cookies. Bryan began to think that he should provide baking services as his "student for hire" job skill.

43. Why did Bryan want to bake the cookies?

    a. To make some money.
    b. To help with the school fund-raiser.
    c. To win a trip to New York City.
    d. To share with his friends.

44. About how old is Bryan in this selection?

    a. 5 years old
    b. 9 years old
    c. 15 years old
    d. 22 years old

45. Why was Bryan unfamiliar with the recipe?

    a. He had never had oatmeal chocolate-chip cookies before.
    b. He didn't like oatmeal chocolate-chip cookies.
    c. He did not know what a recipe was.
    d. He had not baked oatmeal chocolate-chip cookies before.

46. The phrase "fall into place" most closely means

   a. something fell
   b. will work correctly
   c. placed next to
   d. break apart

47. The term "blotted" means

   a. fat
   b. spotted
   c. buttoned
   d. greasy

48. The first step in the directions should be

   a. Work in flour and baking soda to wet mixture.
   b. Last, stir in oats, chocolate chips, and nuts. Mix well.
   c. Next, add eggs, milk, and vanilla. Beat thoroughly.
   d. First, heat oven to 375 degrees F.

49. The second step in the directions should be

   a. Work in flour and baking soda to wet mixture.
   b. Begin by beating butter and sugar until creamy.
   c. Next, add eggs, milk, and vanilla. Beat thoroughly.
   d. First, heat oven to 375 degrees F.

50. The third step in the direction should be

   a. Begin by beating butter and sugar until creamy.
   b. Drop dough onto cookie sheet and bake for 9-10 minutes.
   c. Next, add eggs, milk, and vanilla. Beat thoroughly.
   d. Last, stir in oats, chocolate chips, and nuts. Mix well.

51. The phrase "common sense" could be substituted with

   a. sense of taste
   b. basic thinking skills
   c. cooking skills
   d. imagination

Content Cluster: SPELLING

Objective: To evaluate spelling skills.

> **Parent Tip:** Help your children expand their spelling vocabulary by exposing them to rich print. Reinforce and practice difficult spellings such as **ei** and **ie** words. The format that is often used on standardized tests is what may be most confusing to children with weaker skills. They need to be able to identify both a correctly spelled word as well as a misspelled word. Students with weaker phonics will fall into the traps designed into a test.

Identify the word that is spelled incorrectly:

1.   a. addition   b. addreses   c. administer   d. admonish

2.   a. agricultre   b. access   c. algebra   d. admiral

3.   a. arrangement   b. architecture   c. amusment   d. attention

4.   a. beautiful   b. braged   c. boundary   d. brief

5.   a. biologist   b. brouht   c. businesses   d. bright

6.   a. camra   b. caution   c. chute   d. choose

7.   a. choice   b. clothen   c. cruise   d. crews

8.   a. describe   b. diagram   c. dezign   d. dictionary

9.   a. dought   b. dollar   c. division   d. drawn

10. a. eagre   b. eagle   c. echo   d. electric

11. a. equator   b. envy   c. enviroment   d. explain

12. a. field   b. feirce   c. fault   d. favorite

13. a. fourt   b. flies   c. fragile   d. friendship

14. a. genuine   b. genuis   c. guild   d. geology

15. a. geometry   b. guesess   c. goal   d. grudge

16.	a. happen	b. halfs	c. haven't	d. heir
17.	a. hollow	b. hospital	c. hurried	d. hieght
18.	a. insteed	b. impolite	c. ignorant	d. impossbile
19.	a. infection	b. inguire	c. imperfect	d. illegal
20.	a. justice	b. juree	c. January	d. judge
21.	a. juror	b. jerk	c. jewl	d. jammed
22.	a. knapsac	b. knew	c. knight	d. knot
23.	a. kneer	b. kennel	c. keel	d. kindness
24.	a. laid	b. large	c. layer	d. leafs
25.	a. lecture	b. legth	c. lessons	d. liar
26.	a. license	b. limb	c. lamb	d. loos
27.	a. mission	b. mispell	c. misuse	d. musician
28.	a. miosture	b. months	c. mountain	d. multiply
29.	a. neither	b. nieghbor	c. neglect	d. nurse
30.	a. never	b. nefew	c. niece	d. none
31.	a. obay	b. occasion	c. ocean	d. only
32.	a. often	b. official	c. orcestra	d. oxygen
33.	a. paragraph	b. pickel	c. purse	d. peaceful
34.	a. pasion	b. panic	c. photograph	d. portable
35.	a. quarter	b. quickest	c. quick	d. quist
36.	a. quell	b. qualm	c. quet	d. quite
37.	a. radio	b. raise	c. request	d. rital
38.	a. refferee	b. region	c. regular	d. reign

Content Cluster: LATIN WORD ROOTS

Objective: To evaluate knowledge of word origins, word parts, and their associated meanings.

Parent Tip: Help your children to become familiar with common prefixes and suffixes that will help them analyze a word and determine its meaning from its parts. As students associate meaning to parts of words they know, they are better able to evaluate new words in reading and test taking situations.

Examples:

Common Prefixes and their meanings:
- re – means to "do again" or "from
- un – means "not"
- equa – means "like" or "same"
- dis – means "not"
- de – means "separate"
- mis – means "not" or "wrongly"
- pre – means "before"

Common suffixes and their meanings:
- -er – one who does
- -ful – full of
- -able – able to
- -ship – the condition of
- -ly – in the manner of
- -tion – the state of
- -less – without

Latin word roots:
- spec – means "look" or "sec"
- segregare – means to "separate"
- aequalis – means "get ready"
- port – means "to carry"
- dict – mans "say"
- mot – means "move"

Select the correct word to match the given meaning:

1. Able to be adored

   a. adoring
   b. huggable
   c. adorable
   d. adored

2.　In a willing manner

　　a.　willful
　　b.　wishful
　　c.　willess
　　d.　willingly

3.　Not afraid

　　a.　unafraid
　　b.　afraidful
　　c.　afraidship
　　d.　afraid

4.　Not attractive

　　a.　attractiveless
　　b.　attracting
　　c.　ugly
　　d.　unattractive

5.　The state of being a friend

　　a.　friend
　　b.　friendly
　　c.　friendship
　　d.　friendliest

6.　One who labors

　　a.　laborer
　　b.　labrador
　　c.　laborful
　　d.　laborless

7.　Without fear

　　a.　fearful
　　b.　fearing
　　c.　fearness
　　d.　fearless

8. Able to be carried

   a. carriable
   b. portage
   c. portable
   d. carryful

9. One who teaches

   a. teaching
   b. teach
   c. reach
   d. teacher

10. To say what will happen before

    a. dictionary
    b. preform
    c. predict
    d. predicate

11. One who sees

    a. spectacle
    b. spectacular
    c. specializing
    d. spectator

12. Moved far from

    a. movable
    b. movement
    c. motivation
    d. remote

13. One who says what to do

    a. motivator
    b. dictator
    c. dictionary
    d. motivation

LANGUAGE ARTS
Answer Key

Synonyms
1. c
2. a
3. d
4. b
5. c
6. d
7. a
8. c
9. b
10. d
11. b
12. a
13. d
14. d

Antonyms
1. c
2. d
3. b
4. d
5. d
6. a
7. c
8. a
9. b
10. c
11. d
12. b
13. d
14. a

Context
1. c
2. a

3. c
4. d
5. a
6. c
7. b
8. d
9. a
10. c

Multiple Meanings
1. d
2. d
3. d
4. c
5. b
6. c
7. c

Sentence Structure and Usage
1. c
2. b
3. b
4. c
5. a
6. c
7. b
8. b
9. a

Figurative Language Skills
1. d
2. d
3. b
4. b
5. c
6. d
7. b
8. c
9. b
10. a
11. c
12. d
13. b
14. b

Capitalization and Punctuation
1. c
2. b
3. c
4. c
5. b
6. b
7. b
8. c
9. b

Reading Comprehension
1. c
2. c

3. b
4. c
5. d
6. b
7. b
8. b
9. b
10. b
11. c
12. a
13. c
14. b
15. b
16. b
17. c
18. d
19. b
20. b
21. c
22. b
23. d
24. a
25. d
26. b
27. d
28. c
29. c
30. c
31. b
32. b
33. a
34. d
35. d
36. a
37. b
38. c
39. b
40. a
41. c
42. d
43. b
44. c
45. d
46. b
47. b
48. d
49. b
50. c
51. b

Spelling
1. b
2. a
3. c
4. b
5. b
6. a
7. b
8. c
9. a
10. a
11. c
12. b
13. a
14. b
15. b
16. b
17. d
18. a
19. b

20. b
21. c
22. a
23. a
24. d
25. b
26. d
27. b
28. a
29. b
30. b
31. a
32. c
33. b
34. a
35. d
36. c
37. d
38. a

LatinWord Roots
1. c
2. d
3. a
4. d
5. c
6. a
7. d
8. c
9. d
10. c
11. d
12. d
13. b

MATH

Content Cluster: CONCEPTS/WHOLE NUMBER COMPUTATION

Objective: To evaluate the use of numbers in various mathematical situations and compute them accurately.

Parent Tip: Help your child master his addition, subtraction, multiplication, and division facts. Your child must have strategies to work with larger number concepts such as doubling, estimating, using comfortable numbers, solving a simpler problem first, trial and error, and using number sense. These strategies are discussed in the back of the book.

Example:

A hot air balloon can lift 400 pounds. Steve weighs 110 pounds, Alex weighs 140 pounds, Josè weighs 95 pounds, and Billy weighs 76 pounds. What is their combined weight?

    a. 821
    b. 521
    c. 421
    d. 321

The correct answer is "c". Total the boys' weights. How much the balloon can lift is unnecessary for this problem.

Choose the correct answer:

1. Find the difference between 43,726 and 68,002.

    a. 14,276
    b. 24,276
    c. 70,128
    d. 71,728

2. Mr. Jones collects sports cards. He has 14,115 baseball cards, 8,721 basketball cards, and 487 football cards. How large is his collection?

    a. 150,025
    b. 32,233
    c. 23,323
    d. 17,706

3. Which product is greatest?

   a. 525 x 15
   b. 515 x 20
   c. 500 x 25
   d. 5251 x 5

4. Find the quotient for 4356 ÷ 6.

   a. 826
   b. 726
   c. 626
   d. 526

5. Which equation is true?

   a. 425 x 5 = 848 x 3
   b. 424 x 6 = 708 x 3
   c. 425 x 5 = 708 x 3
   d. 424 x 6 = 848 x 3

6. Which number is the best estimate for the average of 360 x 150?

   a. 5,000
   b. 50,000
   c. 6,500
   d. 8,000

7. What is the difference between 24 and 100?

   a. 76
   b. 124
   c. −76
   d. -124

Content Cluster: NUMBER SENSE AND NUMERATION

Objective: To evaluate place value skills from hundredths to millions. To evaluate an understanding of numbers by applying a sense of reasonableness to a mathematical situation.

Parent Tip: Help your children master their understanding and use of place value. They should be able to construct and use a place value chart from hundredths to millions. Additionally, they must recognize the difference between whole number and decimal values.

Example: Which statement is true?

       a.   69.02 < 6.90
       b.   6.90 > .690
       c.   690. < 69.02
       d.   690 > 690.2

Choose the best answer.

The correct answer is "b". Six and nine-tenths is greater than sixty-nine hundredths. Students must compare each of the number values and then the use of the >,<, or = symbols. They also need to understand the placement and value of zero in whole number and decimal locations.

1. Which set of numbers is listed from greatest to least?

       a.   (84,810   85,810   86,810   87,810)
       b.   (84,100   84,200   84,300   84,400)
       c.   (87,810   86,810   85,810   84,810)
       d.   (84,400   84,300   84,100   84,200)

2. Which number is represented by (6 x 1,000,000) + (4 x 10,000) + (6 x 1000) + (5 x 100) + (6 x 10) + (5 x 1)?

       a.   646,565
       b.   640,565
       c.   6,460,565
       d.   6,046,565

3. Which number has the digit 9 in the ten thousands place?

    a. 6,909,432
    b. 6,090,932
    c. 6,900,932
    d. 9,609,932

4. What is the sum of 864,421 + 1000?

    a. 874,421
    b. 974,421
    c. 865,421
    d. 865,521

5. Which value is the greatest?

    a. 1012.16
    b. 1012.06
    c. 1021.06
    d. 1021.26

6. Which answer is ordered from least to greatest?

    a. 71.02, 7110.2, 7102.11
    b. 111.02, 101.02, 102.01
    c. 31.03, 310.30, 3103.03
    d. 123.4, 102.34, 1234.12

Content Cluster: MEASUREMENT AND GEOMETRY

Objective: To evaluate an understanding of plane and solid geometric shapes by identifying and applying mathematical formulas and solving problems.

Parent Tip: Help your child understand the difference between plane two-dimensional objects and solid three-dimensional geometric objects (square vs. cube). She must be familiar with the vocabulary of geometry such as: faces, edges, vertices, etc., listed in the back of this book. Additionally, she must know the mathematical formulas for perimeter, area, and volume, also listed in the back of this book.

Example: What is the area for the shaded space inside the figure below?

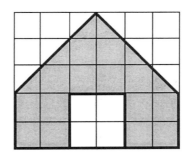

   a. 24 units^2
   b. 17 units^2
   c. 20 units^2
   d. 19 units^2

The correct answer is "b". To get this, you count the total number of shaded squares (14). Then count the shaded triangles (6). Two triangles equal one square unit. So, 14 + 3 = 17

Choose the correct answer:

1. Which figure is <u>congruent</u> to the first?

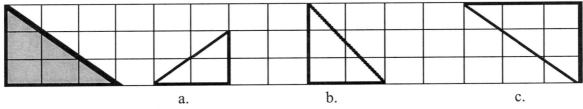

          a.   b.   c.

2. Which shape has a line of symmetry?

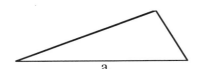
a.

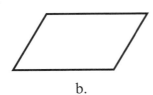
b.

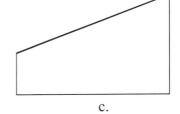
c.

3. Which figure has a measurement of 180°?

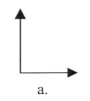
a.

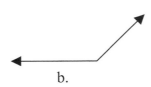
b.

c.

4. Which figure has parallel lines?

a.

b.

c.

5. Which pair of lines are perpendicular?

a.

b.

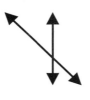
c.

6. Which is the best estimate for the area of the following figure?

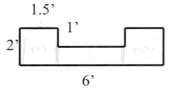

    a. 12 feet^2 b. 16 feet^2 c. 8 feet^2

7. How long is a horizontal line segment with endpoints (-3,2) and (2,2)?

    a.   1
    b.   6
    c.   5

8. What is the radius of a circle with a diameter of 14cm?

    a.   7cm
    b.   24cm
    c.   28cm

9. How many faces does a rectangular prism have?

    a.   none
    b.   12
    c.   6

10. Which figure represents an equilateral triangle?

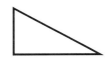

       a.   b.   c.

11. A _____ has 8 edges.

    a.   square
    b.   cube
    c.   pyramid

Content Cluster: STATISTICS AND PROBABILITY

Objective: To evaluate interpretation of numerical data. To evaluate the ability to make predictions for simple probability situations.

Parent Tip: Help your child to interpret different types of graphs and charts. Help him practice using mode, median, range, and average (formulas in glossary). Lastly, he needs to be familiar with expressing outcomes of probability situations numerically (e.g. 3 out of 4; ¾).

Example: At a recent bowling tournament, Steve Star scored 293, 284, 272, 279, and 212 in 5 games. What was his average score?

    a. 279
    b. 268
    c. 272
    d. 270

The correct answer is "b". You must total the 5 scores (1340) and divide by the number of scores (5). The result is 268.

Use the table below for questions 1 through 3.

Candy Store Inventory

	Name of Product	Pieces per Box	# Boxes per Package
a.	Chocolate Raisins	121	12
b.	Chocolate Peanuts	95	12
c.	Cream Caramels	60	24
d.	Luscious Lollys	75	10

1. Which package has the greatest number of total pieces?

    a. Chocolate Raisins
    b. Chocolate Peanuts
    c. Cream Caramels
    d. Luscious Lollys

2. If all candy packages are priced equally, which package has the greatest cost per piece?

    a. Chocolate Raisins
    b. Chocolate Peanuts
    c. Cream Caramels
    d. Luscious Lollys

3. How many boxes of Cream Caramels come in 5 packages?

    a. 100
    b. 1440
    c. 120
    d. 240

Use the following graph to answer questions 4 through 6.

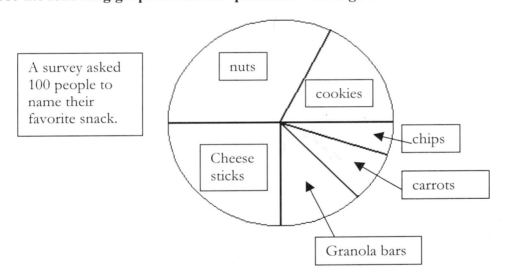

Match each response with the correct percent:

4. Cookies were chosen by:

    a. 50 %   b. 25 %   c. 18 %   d. 35 %

5. Carrots were chosen by:

    a. 4 %   b. 8 %   c. 15 %   d. 22 %

6. Nuts and/or cookies were chosen by:

    a. 32 %   b. 18 %   c. 40 %   d. 50 %

Use the following diagram to answer questions 7 through 10.

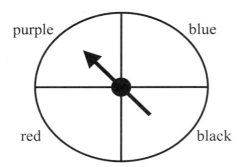

Predict the results of 100 spins.

7. The spinner will land on purple.

    a. 1/10
    b. 50 %
    c. 25/100
    d. 100 %

8. The spinner will land on either purple or black.

    a. 1/10
    b. 50 %
    c. 25/100
    d. 100 %

9. Red has the same chance as:

    a. purple
    b. blue
    c. black
    d. all of the above

10. The spinner has a 3 in 4 chance to land on red, black, and _____ combined.

    a. purple
    b. red
    c. black
    d. none of the above

Content Cluster: FRACTION AND DECIMAL CONCEPTS

Objective: To evaluate the ability to interpret parts of a whole, parts of a set, use division concepts, and relate to decimal values.

Parent Tip: Help children to develop fractional sense by constantly exposing them to units cut or divided into equal parts. Help them see doubling patterns such as halves, quarters, eighths, sixteenths, etc. When working with odd numbered denominators, use a "log" to illustrate the value (such as a loaf of bread). Students too often become focused on boxes and circles for creating fractions and become confused when they have to draw fifths or sevenths. Additionally, they need to become aware of parts of groups. Decimal concepts need to be identified as special fractions that are based on units of 10. Decimals are fractional parts. Using money to create an understanding about hundredth and tenths is most practical.

Example: Identify the portion that is <u>not</u> shaded.

a. 4/10   b. 2/5   c. 3/5   d. 50 %

The correct answer is "c". Six out of 10 boxes are <u>not</u> shaded. The fraction 6/10 is equivalent to 3/5 by reducing to lowest terms.

Choose the correct answer.

1. A large pizza has 12 slices. 2/3 of the pizza has been eaten. How many slices have been eaten?

   a. 2
   b. 3
   c. 7
   d. 8

Use the diagram to answer questions 2 and 3.

2. Look inside the large rectangle. What fraction of the shapes are triangles?

    a. 3/12
    b. 4/4
    c. 1/5
    d. 1/3

3. What fraction of the shapes has straight lines?

    a. 4/12
    b. 1/5
    c. 8/12
    d. 1/3

4. Which decimal has the same value as ¾?

    a. .34
    b. .43
    c. .75
    d. .56

5. Which decimal has the same value as 125/100?

    a. .125
    b. 1.25
    c. 12.5
    d. 125.

Content Cluster: PATTERNS AND RELATIONSHIPS

Objective: To evaluate the ability to analyze patterns and relationships in order to predict the additional items in a series.

Parent Tip: Help your child to analyze the pattern before him. He should look for a visual pattern and draw out what he thinks is next. Or, when using number patterns, he should identify the mathematical equation within the pattern and then apply it.

Example: Fill in the blank.

ABBC, BCCD, _____, DEEF

a. CBBD   b. CDDE   c. DCCE   d. EFFG

The correct answer is "b". The first letter in each item is in alphabetical order, followed by the doubling of the next alphabetical letter, and ending with a single alphabetically ordered letter in the chain.

Choose the correct answer.

1. Which will come next?   18, 36, 72, _____,

 rrect for the following?   2, 8, 20, 44,

next?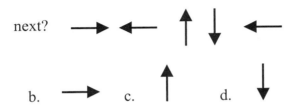

b.   c.   d.

4. Which fraction does not belong in the pattern?   1/5, 2/10, 3/15, 4/25

   a. 1/5   b. 2/10   c. 3/15   d. 4/25

Content Cluster: ESTIMATION

Objective: To evaluate the ability to appropriately estimate mathematical values and solve estimation.

Parent Tip: Help your children to use estimation skills on a regular basis. Estimation skills help to develop a greater math sense. Students may use different estimation strategies depending upon the type of math problem. Traditional rounding may be used with very specific directions such as rounding to the nearest hundred. Larger estimation skills are used in situations that call for an approximate or "about" type answer. Students often use compatible or friendly numbers that make sense to solve a problem. This actually simplifies the math.

Example: Mr. Smith bought 5 cans of dog food at 67¢ each. About how much did they cost all together?

     a. $3.00   b. 70¢   c. $3.50   d. $3.35

The correct answer is "c". When the word "about" is used in a problem, you are being directed to use estimation skills. 67¢ is closest to 70¢. (70¢ x 5 = $3.50)

1. Estimate the quotient for 278 ÷ 4 =

    a. 60
    b. 65
    c. 70
    d. 75

2. Estimate the product for 38 x 18 =

    a. 400
    b. 800
    c. 300
    d. 500

3. About how much will it cost to buy 3 pairs of shoes priced at $39.95, $24.95, and $12.99?

    a. $80.00   b. $70.00   c. $60.00   d. $50.00

4. About how much money should Mrs. Jackson plan to spend if she buys 10 azeala plants at $2.95 each. Be sure she overestimates.

    a. $25.00   b. $30.00   c. $35.00   d. $40.00

Content Cluster: PROBLEM SOLVING STRATEGIES

Objective: To evaluate the ability to analyze a math problem and apply an appropriate problem solving strategy.

Parent Tip: Help your children to solve word problems by getting them to read the question CAREFULLY. They should write out an equation or draw a picture to complement their thinking. When in doubt, draw it out! Creating a visual can be of monumental assistance, especially to students who struggle in the language area. Additionally, they need to work through a problem using _their_ thinking style rather than always having to follow traditional equations. The way math was taught to you 20 to 30 years ago is not the way that students have to solve math today.

Strong basic skills will help build success in problem solving. By the fourth grade, math problems involve large numbers, and if students are struggling with the basic facts, they may feel frustrated with multiple step problems.

Example:

Jenny is raising mice for a science experiment. She has a total of 36 mice in a small and large cage. The large cage has double the number of mice. How many are in the small cage?

    a. 24   b. 36   c. 18   d. 12

The correct answer is "d". The small cage has 12 while the large has 24. 24 is double 12 and their sum is 36.

1. Samantha had 3 types of meat: turkey, roast beef, and ham. She had 2 types of bread: white and wheat. How many sandwich choices are there if there is only one type of meat per sandwich?

    a. 3
    b. 6
    c. 9
    d. 12

2. Juanita enjoys bike riding. She rides at a rate of 2.5 miles every 10 minutes. If she rides steadily at this rate how far will she go in a ½ hour?

    a. 25 miles
    b. 15 miles
    c. 7.5 miles
    d. 9.5 miles

3. Kathy decided to give away her coin collection. She sold 124 coins, then equally divided the rest among her 3 sisters. They each got 69. How many coins had been in Kathy's collection?

   a. 331
   b. 207
   c. 173
   d. 176

4. A 1 pound package of chocolate candies has 48 pieces. 1/6 of them are caramels, 1/3 have nuts, and ½ are either light or dark solids. How many have nuts?

   a. 8
   b. 16
   c. 12
   d. 20

5. At Public School #111, the milk is sold in ½ pint containers. On an average day, the school sells 632 containers. How many gallons of milk is that?

   a. 390
   b. 39.5
   c. 316
   d. 158

Content Cluster: LOGIC AND PROBLEM SOLVING

Objective: To evaluate knowledge of problem solving strategies that involve pre-algebraic thinking and multiple-step procedures.

Parent Tip: Help your children to feel successful when approaching word problems by having them draw or list parts of the problem. Many students have difficulty with these types of problems because they are not the basis of many math programs. However, they are just the type of problem that students will encounter in tests of math skills. Students quickly become better at these problems as they try more and more of them. At times, students can solve problems without traditional equations; however, the stronger their basic math skills and math sense, the more likely they are to solve these problems.

Children should be familiar with such strategies as working backwards, solving a simpler problem first, trial and error, and logical estimation. They also need to have a strong math vocabulary to analyze and understand what some questions are asking.

Choose the correct answer.

1. When a clock reads 10:15, what time would it read if you were looking into a mirror?

   a. 10:15
   b. 11:15
   c. 1:45
   d. 11:45

2. If you have twelve squares, you can arrange them to make three different types of rectangular shapes. (For example: 12 x 1; 6 x 2; and 3 x 4). How many squares would you need in order to make 4 different rectangular shapes?

   a. 4
   b. 16
   c. 24
   d. 36

3. Which of the following is a prime number?

   a. 24
   b. 67
   c. 33
   d. 21

4. If everyone in a class of 20 students shakes hands with everyone else just once, how many handshakes were there?

    a. 19
    b. 63
    c. 190
    d. 400

5. A chime on a clock strikes one chime at one o'clock, two chimes at two o'clock, up to twelve chimes at twelve o'clock. What is the total number of chimes that a clock will strike during a twelve-hour period?

    a. 60
    b. 66
    c. 72
    d. 78

6. Which two consecutive numbers will total 225?

    a. 100 and 125
    b. 110 and 115
    c. 112 and 113
    d. 120 and 105

7. How many cubes are necessary to build the figure below, if the figure is solid?

    a. 24
    b. 48
    c. 60
    d. 72

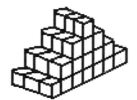

8. Read the clues and find the number:

    The number has three digits.
    The tens digit is one-half the hundreds digit.
    The number is odd.
    The sum of the digits is nine.

a. 243
b. 216
c. 621
d. 423

9. Arrange the digits 2, 4, 7, and 9 so that you get the largest possible product.

    a. 97 x 24
    b. 94 x 72
    c. 92 x 74
    d. 79 x 42

10. If you start with one whole and you cut the pieces in half repeatedly three times, how much do you have?

    a. two halves
    b. three thirds
    c. four quarters
    d. eight eighths

11. Suzanne has six times as many marbles as Kathy. John has half as many as Judy. Judy has half as many as Suzanne. Kathy has four marbles. How many marbles do John and Suzanne have together?

    a. 16
    b. 24
    c. 30
    d. 36

12. The sum of the digits of an odd two-digit prime number is 11. The tens digit is greater than the ones digit. What is the number?

    a. 92
    b. 47
    c. 83
    d. 38

13. A baker is getting ready for the day. He is mixing a very large amount of batter to be able to make several cakes throughout the day. If he splits the batter once, he now has two batches. If he splits those two batches he will then have four. If he continues this process four more times, how many batches of batter will he have?

    a. 6
    b. 16
    c. 30
    d. 64

14. Freddie keeps all his socks in one drawer. He has seven blue socks and nine brown socks. If he reaches in the drawer without looking, what is the fewest number of socks he can take out to be sure of getting a pair of the same color?

    a. 2
    b. 3
    c. 5
    d. 16

15. If it is 10:00 p.m. in California, what time is it in New York City?

    a. 7:00 p.m.
    b. 1:00 a.m.
    c. 1:00 p.m.
    d. 7:00 a.m.

16. A farmer had 457 milk cows. He lost all but 112 of them to disease. How many were left alive?

    a. 369
    b. 112
    c. 569
    d. 445

17. Andy's plant and garden shop sells four rose bushes for every three gardenias. Last month, they sold 48 roses bushes. How many gardenias were sold?

    a. 48
    b. 18
    c. 12
    d. 36

18. Mrs. Johnson had baked ¾ of the cookies she needed for the bake sale. What percentage of the cookies had she baked?

    a. 20 %
    b. 25 %
    c. 65 %
    d. 75 %

19. Complete the pattern: 1, 1, 2, 3, 5, 8, ___, ___, ___

    a. 15, 17, 19
    b. 12, 17, 23
    c. 13, 21, 34
    d. 13, 22, 35

Content Cluster: MATH COMPUTATION

Objective: To evaluate computation skills using the four operations, fractions, decimals, and percentages.

Parent Tip: To be successful in basic computation, your child must know her addition, subtraction, multiplication, and division facts with complete accuracy. Most errors are the result of calculation mistakes based on inadequate knowledge of facts. Review the procedures for large multiplication, long division, adding and subtracting fractions, working with decimals, and percentages. Repeated practice helps improve accuracy. Additionally, encourage your child to develop her "math sense." This means to evaluate an answer to determine if the answer is logical for the problem. Try to have your child consistently compare her answer back to the original question. Estimation skills are also highly valuable as well.

Students also need to know the following terms:

sum	difference
product	quotient
decimal value	fractional value
mixed number	improper fraction
simplest terms	equivalent fractions
average	percentage

The math glossary for this unit will provide resource information for required vocabulary.

Solve the following and choose the correct answer.

1. Find the product for 432 x 28.

    a. 4320
    b. 4520
    c. 12,096
    d. 11,096

2. What is the difference for 18,642 and 12, 946?

    a. 5696
    b. 5606
    c. 6696
    d. 6606

3. Find the sum for 836 + 12,666 + 42 =

    a. 100,466
    b. 98,042
    c. 13,544
    d. 12,534

4. Find the quotient for 836 divided by 9.

    a. 90 r.9
    b. 91 r.9
    c. 92 r.8
    d. 93 r.8

5. Which equation shows calculating an average?

    a. 98(76 + 89 + 44) x 4 =
    b. (98 + 76 + 89 + 44) ÷ 4 =
    c. (98 + 76) ÷ (89 + 44) =
    d. (98 + 76 + 89 + 44) x 4 =

6. Solve 5672 ÷ 24 =

    a. 226 r.10
    b. 236 r.8
    c. 246 r.10
    d. 256 r.8

7. How much is 25 % of 4?

    a. 1
    b. 4
    c. 8
    d. 16

8. 75 % of 800 =

    a. 800
    b. 700
    c. 600
    d. 500

9. If you score 18/25 on a test your grade would be:

    a. 90 %
    b. 82 %
    c. 80 %
    d. 72 %

10. Solve and name in simplest terms: 5/9 + 6/9 =

    a. 1 1/9
    b. 1 1/5
    c. 1 1/3
    d. 1 2/9

11. Solve and name in simplest terms: 12/15 – 1/3 =

    a. 11/12
    b. 17/15
    c. 7/15
    d. 13/18

12. Complete the pattern: 2/6, 5/15, 9/27, _____

    a. 9/27
    b. 10/33
    c. 11/22
    d. 12/36

13. Solve 450 x 0.5 =

    a. 225
    b. 900
    c. 2250
    d. 1250

14. At the store Sam buys three calculators for $2.99 each. There is no tax. If he pays
    with a twenty-dollar bill, how much change will he receive?

    a. (8) $1.00 bills, (1) $5.00 bill, 2 quarters, and 3 pennies
    b. (2) $5.00 bills, (1) $1.00 bill, and 3 pennies
    c. (1) $10.00 bill, (3) $1.00 bills, and 1 penny
    d. (11) $1.00 bills, and 11 pennies

15. Solve 1215 ÷ _____ = 135

    a.　135
    b.　7
    c.　8
    d.　9

16. Solve 456 x _____ = 5472

    a.　10
    b.　11
    c.　12
    d.　13

17. Use compatible numbers to estimate 42 x 311 =

    a.　120
    b.　1200
    c.　12,000
    d.　120,000

18. ½ x ½ = is the same as

    a.　½
    b.　¼
    c.　1/6
    d.　1/8

19. ¼ of 300 =

    a.　110
    b.　100
    c.　95
    d.　75

20. Mrs. Sylvester went shopping at Mark's Department Store and spent $112.50.　She had to pay 10 % sales tax as well.　Her total bill was:

    a.　$123.75
    b.　$135.50
    c.　$124.50
    d.　$124.00

MATH
Answer Key

20

Concepts/Whole Number Computation

1. b
2. c
3. d
4. b
5. d
6. b
7. a

Number Sense and Numeration

1. c
2. d
3. b
4. c
5. d
6. c

Measurement and Geometry

1. c
2. b
3. c
4. b
5. a
6. c
7. c
8. a
9. c
10. b
11. c

Statistics and Probability

1. a
2. d
3. c
4. c
5. b
6. d
7. c
8. b
9. d
10. a

Fraction and Decimal Concepts

1. d
2. d
3. c
4. c
5. b

Patterns and Relationships

1. c
2. d
3. b
4. d

Estimation

1. c
2. b
3. a
4. b

Problem Solving Strategies

1. b
2. c
3. a
4. b
5. b

Logic and Problem Solving

1. c
2. c
3. b
4. c
5. d
6. c
7. b
8. d
9. c
10. d
11. c
12. c
13. d
14. b
15. b
16. b
17. d
18. d
19. c

Math Computation

1. c
2. a
3. c
4. c
5. b
6. b
7. a
8. c
9. d
10. d
11. c
12. d
13. a
14. b
15. d
16. c
17. c
18. b
19. d
20. a

SOCIAL STUDIES

Content Cluster: PHYSICAL AND GEOGRAPHIC FEATURES

Objective: To evaluate knowledge and use of general map skills, knowledge of world geography, and knowledge of California geography and the significance of each of its regions.

Parent Tip: Help your children to practice reading maps, charts, and pictures related to geography. They should be able to use a variety of grid systems, particularly latitude and longitude. Their basic sense of world geography should include the continents, four hemispheres, the poles, and major land features. Additionally, California geography skills should include knowledge of the regions, land features, and their impact on the economic development of the state.

Choose the correct answer.

1. The continent of _____ is located in both the southern and eastern hemispheres.

   a. North America
   b. Australia
   c. Africa
   d. Europe

2. The equator is located at _____.

   a. 90° latitude
   b. 90° longitude
   c. 0° latitude
   d. 0° longitude

3. The Prime Meridian is a line of

   a. latitude.
   b. longitude.
   c. symmetry.
   d. parallel.

4.   90 degrees N latitude locates the

   a.   North Pole.
   b.   South Pole.
   c.   Equator.
   d.   Prime Meridian.

5.   Two states that border California are

   a.   Arizona and Mexico.
   b.   Mexico and Nevada.
   c.   Arizona and Nevada.
   d.   Colorado and Nevada.

6.   _____ is the capital of California.

   a.   San Francisco
   b.   San Diego
   c.   Modesto
   d.   Sacramento

7.   California is divided into the following regions:

   a.   desert, mountain, coast, and valley.
   b.   desert, mountain, hill, and valley.
   c.   mountains, coast, and valley.
   d.   valley and coast.

8.   The central valley produces

   a.   borax mining.
   b.   gold.
   c.   fruits and vegetables.
   d.   film and television.

9.   Coastal California cities are known for

   a.   borax mining.
   b.   gold .
   c.   fruits and vegetables.
   d.   film and television.

10. Palm Springs, Indio, and Lancaster are found in

    a. coastal areas.
    b. the central valley.
    c. the mountains.
    d. the desert.

11. Lake Tahoe is a natural feature in this region.

    a. central valley
    b. mountains
    c. hills and valleys
    d. desert

12. The mountains of California are sources for these businesses.

    a. aviation and jewelry production
    b. fishing and computers
    c. skiing and gravel excavation
    d. poultry and dairy farms

13. Yosemite is a

    a. lake.
    b. mountain.
    c. park.
    d. canyon.

14. Cities such as Monterey and San Jose developed as a result of their

    a. climate.
    b. rich soil.
    c. coastal location.
    d. surf.

15. Death Valley is located in

    a. Yosemite National Park.
    b. Redwood National Forest.
    c. Palm Springs.
    d. Mojave Desert.

Content Cluster: SOCIAL, POLITICAL, CULTURAL, AND ECONOMIC DEVELOPMENT OF CALIFORNIA FROM ITS ORIGINS THROUGH THE MEXICAN RANCHO PERIOD.

Objective: To evaluate the knowledge of the social, political, cultural, and economic relationships as California developed from pre-Columbian societies through the Mexican rancho period.

Parent Tip: Help your children to understand the cause and effect relationships among a variety of events in history. Your children should recognize the connections between geography and economic development. Your children should be able to identify the cultural influences of different groups in California history.

Choose the correct answer.

1. A northeastern coastal Indian tribe of California was the

    a. Mojave.
    b. Miwok.
    c. Yurok.
    d. Gabrielino.

2. A southwestern desert Indian tribe of California was the

    a. Mojave.
    b. Miwok.
    c. Yurok.
    d. Gabrielino.

3. The Chumash Indians lived near present day

    a. San Diego.
    b. Santa Clara.
    c. Santa Barbara.
    d. San Juan Capistrano.

4. Coastal Indians ate _____ to survive.

    a. squirrels and foxes
    b. clams and fish
    c. cactus and berries
    d. buffalo and deer

5. The Mojave Indians lived by the _____ River.

    a. San Joaquin
    b. Sacramento
    c. Red
    d. Colorado

6. Every tribe's way of life depended on the _____ of the region where it lived.

    a. natural resources
    b. rivers
    c. animals
    d. people

7. Many Indian legends explain nature through the use of

    a. death.
    b. spirits.
    c. toads.
    d. resources.

8. Many Indian tribes _____ for different items.

    a. paid
    b. danced
    c. traded
    d. All the above.

9. Indian ceremonies often focused on the cycle of _____.

    a. fruit
    b. death
    c. life
    d. energy

10. _____ was the Spanish explorer credited with claiming the territory now called California for Spain.

    a. Sir Francis Drake
    b. Juan Cabrillo
    c. Cabeza de Vaca
    d. Arroz con Pollo

11. When the Spanish discovered California, they were actually seeking

   a. Indians.
   b. Gold and riches.
   c. Water.
   d. Food.

12. Spain's interest in California was threatened by

   a. England and the United States.
   b. United States.
   c. Russia and England.
   d. France and England.

13. Father Serra brought _____ to the Indians.

   a. food
   b. clothing
   c. Christianity
   d. water

14. The first of the Spanish missions was located at

   a. San Francisco.
   b. San Diego.
   c. San Juan Capistrano.
   d. San Miguel.

15. The missions were designed to be a _____ apart.

   a. a day's journey
   b. a week's journey
   c. a month's journey
   d. a year's journey

16. Father Serra selected the mission at _____ as his headquarters.

   a. San Gabriel
   b. San Juan Capistrano
   c. San Francisco
   d. Monterey Bay

17. The missions depended upon the labor and skills of the _____.

   a. Spanish
   b. Californios
   c. Americans
   d. Indians

18. Many Indians _____ to the missions to show their anger.

   a. complained
   b. set fire
   c. resisted going
   d. happily went

19. The term presidio means

   a. town.
   b. church.
   c. mission.
   d. fort.

20. The term pueblo means

   a. town.
   b. church.
   c. mission.
   d. fort.

21. The term rancho means

   a. town.
   b. ranch.
   c. mission.
   d. fort.

22. The economy of the missions centered around

   a. hunting.
   b. agriculture.
   c. trading.
   d. weaving.

23. A cause of the Mexican War for Independence was

    a. unfair trade with the U.S.
    b. restrictions about religion.
    c. unequal treatment for Mexican born citizens.
    d. illegal immigration laws.

24. A result of the Mexican War for Independence was

    a. the missions were closed.
    b. the Spanish continued to send trading ships.
    c. the English returned home.
    d. future missions were planned.

25. A _____ was a land map that marked off a rancho.

    a. treaty
    b. grid
    c. diseño
    d. distance

26. Secularization of the missions put them in the hands of

    a. the padres.
    b. the Spanish.
    c. the Mexicans.
    d. the Indians.

27. Ranchos relied upon _____ as the central component of their economy.

    a. Indians
    b. cattle
    c. soap
    d. houses

28. During the rancho period, trading ships from _____ came to California.

    a. Spain
    b. England
    c. Russia
    d. England, Russia, and the United States

Content Cluster: THE ECONOMIC, SOCIAL, AND POLITICAL LIFE OF CALIFORNIA FROM THE BEAR FLAG REPUBLIC TO STATEHOOD.

Objective: To evaluate knowledge of the elements that has changed California from the beginning of the Bear Flag Republic to its acceptance as a state.

Parent Tip: Help your children to understand the "Time-Line" components of major events during this part of California's history. Take note of cause and effect relationships such as the discovery of gold and the boom development of San Francisco.

Choose the correct answer.

1. Jedediah Smith was known as a

   a. fisherman.
   b. trapper.
   c. climber.
   d. soldier.

2. How was Jedediah Smith's journey across the Sierra Nevada significant?

   a. It showed others that there were many beavers in California.
   b. It led the way to friendly relationships with the Californios.
   c. It showed that there was an overland route to California from the United States.
   d. It established a sea route from Boston to San Francisco.

3. Smith was _____ by Mexican officials.

   a. eagerly welcomed
   b. ordered to leave
   c. encouraged to settle
   d. hired as a translator

4. Abel Sterns, also a pioneer, established a(n) _____ business in Los Angeles.

   a. sailing
   b. education
   c. transportation
   d. trading

5. Abel Sterns was accepted by the Mexican government because

    a. he respected the Mexican government.
    b. he was willing to become a Mexican citizen.
    c. he helped improve trading methods for the Californios.
    d. All of the above.

6. Why did John Sutter's settlement grow?

    a. It was a safe place for Spanish padres ousted from the missions.
    b. It became an important stop for travelers from the United States.
    c. It had rich soil.
    d. The Mexican government wanted it to expand.

7. The Donner Party experienced _____ on their way to California.

    a. tragedy
    b. adventure
    c. death
    d. All of the above.

8. The Donner Party experience reminded people that

    a. California had great riches to offer.
    b. getting to the gold rush was worth it all.
    c. it was important to travel cross-country in large groups.
    d. westward travel was still dangerous.

9. The Bear Flag revolt signaled

    a. unrest by settlers from the United States.
    b. threat by large groups of wandering bears.
    c. unrest by Mexican soldiers.
    d. threat by trappers.

10. The Bear Flag rebels wanted California to be

    a. part of the United States.
    b. part of Mexico.
    c. part of England.
    d. an independent state.

11. The United States during the 1840's wanted California to be

    a. part of the United States.
    b. part of Mexico.
    c. part of England.
    d. an independent state.

12. The United States initiated war against Mexico because

    a. they wanted all lands east of the Sierra Nevada.
    b. they wanted all lands owned by Mexico.
    c. they wanted all lands between the east coast and the west coast.
    d. they wanted the Texas territory.

13. Most of the Mexican War was fought in

    a. California and Texas.
    b. Texas and Arizona.
    c. California and Mexico.
    d. Mexico and Texas.

14. The agreement that ended the U.S. – Mexican War was called the

    a. Treaty of Peace.
    b. Treaty of Guadalupe Hidalgo.
    c. Treaty of San Juan Bautista.
    d. Treaty of California.

15. Life in California

    a. remained generally unchanged following the end of the Mexican War.
    b. became Americanized following the end of the Mexican War.
    c. changed drastically following the Mexican War.
    d. was busy and hectic following the end of the Mexican War.

16. James Marshall found pieces of gold at

    a. San Jose.
    b. Sutter's Mill.
    c. Steven's Station.
    d. The Colorado River.

17. Sutter's Fort was located near the modern day city of

    a. San Diego.
    b. Los Angeles.
    c. Santa Barbara.
    d. San Francisco.

18. The Gold Rush began in

    a. 1847.
    b. 1848.
    c. 1849.
    d. 1850.

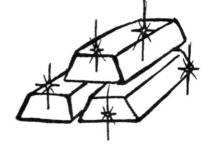

19. The term for daring gold seekers was

    a. Gold Rushers.
    b. Gold Diggers.
    c. Forty-Niners.
    d. Broncos.

20. Which of the following was a method of gold mining?

    a. Panning.
    b. Rocking.
    c. Digging.
    d. All of the above.

21. Life for many gold miners was

    a. full of riches.
    b. exciting and encouraging.
    c. full of hardships.
    d. easy and pleasant.

22. The Gold Rush changed the face of California because

    a. miners had dug holes looking for gold.
    b. miners stayed in California and increased the population.
    c. Mexican settlers left California.
    d. gold dust sparkled in the California hills.

23. The California Gold Rush brought diversity to California

    a. by having different types of mining equipment.
    b. through the increase in Mexican population.
    c. through the increase in Chinese and South American populations.
    d. by decreasing Native Americans in the territory.

24. During the years of the Gold Rush, northern California experienced

    a. positive growth and development due to increased job opportunities.
    b. decreased growth due to limited job opportunities.
    c. planned community growth with quality housing.
    d. increased crime due to frustrations from broken dreams.

25. During the Gold Rush, San Francisco

    a. developed into a well designed city.
    b. suffered from overcrowding and filth.
    c. developed a well organized police system.
    d. was selected the capital by Californios.

26. The end of the Gold Rush brought about _____ between the Californios and the Americans.

    a. peace
    b. cooperation
    c. tension
    d. war

27. How did the constitutional convention change California?

    a. It proclaimed all Mexican land was now the California territory.
    b. It split California into two sections.
    c. It elected Robert Semple governor of the territory.
    d. It determined that the Sierra Nevada Mountains and the Colorado River would become its natural boundaries.

28. The size of the California territory was determined

    a. to be fair to the Californios.
    b. based upon the ability to control it.
    c. based upon the treaty of the Mexican War.
    d. to be fair to the Americans.

29. California had to wait a year to become a state because of its position on

   a. voting rights.
   b. state size.
   c. slavery.
   d. Native American rights.

30. Biddy Mason is remembered for

   a. her work to improve the education of black children.
   b. working hard and saving money to get ahead.
   c. having been a female slave who later owned her own home.
   d. All of the above.

31. A vigilante

   a. lawfully assists the local police.
   b. unlawfully assists the local police.
   c. disregards all laws related to justice.
   d. has great regard for the law of the land.

32. Why were the Californios unable to keep squatters from taking their land?

   a. The squatters outnumbered the Californios.
   b. The squatters had the law on their side.
   c. The squatters were supported by the state constitution.
   d. The squatters were acting on behalf of the U.S. government.

33. How did the Land Commission hurt the Californios?

   a. They usually ruled in favor of the ranchero.
   b. They did not listen to the rancher's claim.
   c. They took many years to issue their decision.
   d. They did not follow the laws that protected the ranchero's rights.

Content Cluster: CALIFORNIA'S ECONOMIC DEVELOPMENT (POST 1850s) INTO AN AGRICULTURAL AND INDUSTRIAL POWER.

Objective: To evaluate knowledge of technological advances (Pony Express, Western Union, and Transcontinental Railroad) that connected California to the rest of the U.S. To evaluate knowledge of California's development as an economically diverse state with a multi-cultural population that has successfully evolved during the last 150 years.

Parent Tip: Help your child to understand the more recent developments in California's history. Many schools do not cover the entire time line of California's history, and instead focus on a few major events. This section covers areas that your child is less likely to be familiar with such as immigration, effects of the Great Depression and World War II, development of new industries, cultural development, and important 20th century Californians.

Choose the correct answer.

1. When California entered the Union, it's greatest weakness was

   a. it was a non-slave state.
   b. it had allowed women to own land.
   c. it was physically isolated from much of the United States.
   d. it lacked natural resources.

2. Why was the Pony Express important to California?

   a. It brought national news to them at a much faster rate.
   b. It let them send letters to people in other places.
   c. It gave them a purpose to raise quality horses.
   d. It brought packages to them.

3. What solution did the Californian's come up with to reduce transportation costs?

   a. expansion of the Pony Express
   b. use of the telegraph
   c. expansion of wagon trains
   d. building a transcontinental railroad

4. During the Civil War, food and supplies went to soldiers. What effect did this have on California?

   a. They produced their own food.
   b. They felt cut off from the rest of the United States.
   c. They helped to send food and supplies to the soldiers.
   d. They started a new trade business with Russia.

5. Theodore Judah could be called the

   a. Father of the Transcontinental Railroad.
   b. Mountaineer of the Sierra Nevada.
   c. Designer of Dreams.
   d. American Architect

6. One of the greatest obstacles to building the transcontinental railroad was

   a. the Colorado River.
   b. acquiring money.
   c. the U.S. government.
   d. the people of California.

7. Why did many of the original railroad laborers abandon their jobs?

   a. The Gold Rush
   b. Silver was found in Nevada.
   c. Disease was spreading among the workers.
   d. Lack of money

8. Who helped to continue and finish the railroad?

   a. Native American laborers
   b. Mexican laborers
   c. Chinese laborers
   d. South American laborers

9. At the end of the Gold Rush, many miners turned to _____ to make a living.

   a. fishing
   b. farming
   c. logging
   d. trading

10. By 1870, _____ was California's most important crop.

  a. fish
  b. strawberries
  c. wheat
  d. oats

11. Which of the following contributed to California's agricultural development?

  a. advances in farm machinery
  b. improvements in irrigation
  c. transportation
  d. All of the above.

12. Canneries were operated by

  a. Native Americans, Americans, and Californios
  b. Irish, Italian, Chinese, and Mexican immigrants
  c. Russian, English, and Spanish immigrants
  d. All of the above.

13. This development helped to make California one of the top agricultural producers to the United States.

  a. Telegraph
  b. Telephone
  c. Refrigeration
  d. Dehydration

14. Southern California grew during the late 1800s as a result of

  a. interest in the southern beaches.
  b. interest in grapes.
  c. interest in oranges.
  d. interest in avocados.

15. _____ between the Santa Fe and Southern Pacific Railroads helped Southern California grow.

  a. Cooperation
  b. Competition
  c. Creativity
  d. Comparison

16. Thirty years after the gold rush, southern California was in a

    a. depression.
    b. bust.
    c. decline.
    d. boom.

17. Many California farmers had difficulty with water. Their solutions included

    a. dams.
    b. aqueducts.
    c. reservoirs.
    d. All of the above.

18. California attracted immigrants from many places because

    a. it had a reputation as a land of wealth and opportunity.
    b. it encouraged immigrants to come there.
    c. immigrants were given jobs when they arrived.
    d. All of the above.

19. Solvang, California was settled by

    a. Asian immigrants.
    b. Swiss immigrants.
    c. Japanese immigrants.
    d. German immigrants.

20. Los Angeles has a large

    a. European community.
    b. Japanese and Korean community.
    c. Portugese community.
    d. Russian community.

21. The development of the car helped the development of the _____industry in California.

    a. steel
    b. paint
    c. oil
    d. light bulb

22. The creation of the Panama Canal helped boost _____ with California.

    a. relationships
    b. trade
    c. irrigation
    d. agriculture

23. During the 1930s, California became a destination for families from Dust Bowl states as well as those trying to escape the effects of the depression. This created

    a. an increase in soil build up throughout California.
    b. an increase in population throughout California.
    c. a decrease in population throughout California.
    d. an increase in the entertainment industry.

24. How did President Roosevelt's New Deal affect California?

    a. The New Deal put people to work in big construction projects.
    b. The New Deal began the construction of Las Vegas.
    c. The New Deal provided opportunity for building swimming pools.
    d. The New Deal built movie studios.

25. What effect did the building of the San Pedro Harbor and the Panama Canal have on California?

    a. It made San Francisco a major seaport.
    b. It made Monterey a major seaport.
    c. It made Los Angeles a major seaport.
    d. It made San Diego a major seaport.

26. When World War II broke out, why did it produce greater fear in Californians?

    a. There were many Japanese-Americans living in California who might revolt.
    b. Californians thought they would be bombed next due to their location.
    c. They were concerned that waterways would collapse.
    d. They were concerned that oil production would decrease.

27. Pilot Chuck Yeager made history at Edwards Air Force Base in 1947 when he

    a. flew around the United States.
    b. flew an X-1 at supersonic speed and broke the sound barrier.
    c. flew a stealth bomber for the first time ever.
    d. flew an F-14 bomber over Japan.

28. The term aerospace refers to

    a. the technology used to design aircraft.
    b. the technology used to build aircraft.
    c. the technology used to fly aircraft.
    d. All of the above.

29. Following WWII, California developed a strong reputation for

    a. chemical engineering.
    b. physical engineering.
    c. aerospace engineering.
    d. financial engineering.

30. The California Institute of Technology helped develop _____ that carried astronauts to the moon.

    a. tiles
    b. rockets
    c. food
    d. fuel

31. How did California farming change in the years following WWII?

    a. Cures for plant diseases were discovered at California universities.
    b. Specialized farm machinery was developed at California universities.
    c. Faster farm machinery was developed at California universities.
    d. All of the above.

32. In the 1980s, California's Silicon Valley became well known for

    a. the San Francisco 49'ers.
    b. farming and mining.
    c. computers and technology.
    d. agriculture and recreation.

33. Why did large numbers of immigrants come to California after 1965?

    a. The governor of California advertised for people to come from other countries.
    b. Television and radio programs promoted California to foreign countries.
    c. As part of a trade agreement with Europe and Asia, families were asked to move to California.
    d. The U.S. government passed the 1965 immigration law that created new opportunities for emigrating people.

34. Why did many new immigrants come from Pacific Rim countries?

    a. They liked the California climate.
    b. Pacific Rim countries did not have a direct route to California.
    c. The immigrants liked the food in the California.
    d. There were many dangers in Pacific Rim countries during the 1960s and 70s.

35. During the past 25 years, California has continued to grow due to

    a. technology.
    b. trade.
    c. education.
    d. All of the above.

36. Today, some of California's leading exports are

    a. hides and tallow.
    b. ice cream and candy.
    c. milk and bananas.
    d. computers and films.

37. California has the largest system of higher education in the United States. This statement supports that

    a. state leaders and businessmen value well-educated citizens.
    b. education beyond high school is important for California's growth and progress.
    c. people of all backgrounds should have a chance at a good education.
    d. All of the above.

38. In 1960, California passed a law that changed its university system. This law

    a. said that only people who could afford to pay could go to California universities.
    b. stated that you must be born in California to go to one of its universities.
    c. supported the idea that all people with good grades should go on to higher education regardless of their economic background.
    d. allowed for everybody to go to universities and colleges if they wanted to.

39. The entertainment industry is a central part of California's economic success. Which of the following people earned a world-wide reputation for innovative ideas about animation?

    a. John Wayne
    b. Walt Disney
    c. John Steinbeck
    d. Ansel Adams

40. Which Californian is known for contributions to literature?

    a. John Wayne
    b. Walt Disney
    c. John Steinbeck
    d. Ansel Adams

41. Which Californian is known for contributions to photography and art?

    a. John Wayne
    b. Walt Disney
    c. John Steinbeck
    d. Ansel Adams

42. Which Californian is well known for early movie productions?

    a. Louis B. Meyer
    b. Neil Armstrong
    c. Ansel Adams
    d. Pete Wilson

43. Water has always been a crucial issue for people living in certain parts of California. What effect did the Los Angeles aqueduct have on the Owens Valley?

    a. Cattle are plentiful in the rich valley.
    b. Agriculture flourishes in the valley.
    c. Fields have an irrigation system in the Owens Valley.
    d. Dust storms have become common across the valley.

Content Cluster: THE STRUCTURE, FUNCTION, AND POWERS OF LOCAL, STATE, AND NATIONAL GOVERNMENTS.

Objective: To evaluate knowledge of basic systems and principals of our state and federal governing systems in the United States.

Parent Tip: Help your children to understand the three branches of government and their individual roles as well as their integrated roles in a system of checks and balances. Be sure your children are aware of the differences between local, state, and national governments and that the term "federal" refers to the national government.

Choose the correct answer.

1. The U.S. Constitution provides

    a. a description for three branches of government at different (local, state, and national) levels.
    b. a letter from Thomas Jefferson about the role of government.
    c. all levels of government with equal and same powers.
    d. a structure for business opportunities.

2. Which branch of government is responsible for making laws?

    a. Executive
    b. Judicial
    c. Legislative
    d. Historical

3. Which branch of government is responsible for interpreting laws?

    a. Executive
    b. Judicial
    c. Legislative
    d. Historical

4. Which branch of government is responsible for seeing that laws are carried out?

    a. Executive
    b. Judicial
    c. Legislative
    d. Historical

5. The term "federal" refers to government at the _____ level.

   a. district
   b. local
   c. state
   d. national

6. A system of "checks and balances" refers to

   a. a banking or budgeting method.
   b. three branches of laws.
   c. three branches of government.
   d. a way to weigh or measure the importance of a law.

7. The leader of the federal government is the

   a. President.
   b. Governor.
   c. Mayor.
   d. City Council.

8. The leader of state government is the

   a. President.
   b. Governor.
   c. Mayor.
   d. City Council.

9. State governments are given power to

   a. legislate laws related to the environment in their own state.
   b. overrule federal laws.
   c. print their own money.
   d. change federal laws.

10. State governments are denied the power to

   a. create laws to protect their environment.
   b. declare war and keep their own armies.
   c. establish traffic laws.
   d. establish recycling programs.

11. The federal government is similar to state governments in that they both

    a. have three branches of government.
    b. create new laws.
    c. interpret laws.
    d. All of the above.

12. In California, one of the state government jobs is to control

    a. treaties with foreign countries.
    b. pollution.
    c. printing of money.
    d. taxation of imports.

13. Each state elects _____ United States Senators.

    a. two
    b. four
    c. six
    d. eight

14. It is the responsibility of the federal government to

    a. feed all people.
    b. clothe all people.
    c. educate all people.
    d. defend all people from attack by other countries.

15. The President of the United States is the leader of the nation's

    a. environmental protection group.
    b. congressional committees.
    c. military forces.
    d. national choir.

Content Cluster: MAP SKILLS

Objective: To demonstrate knowledge of world and state geography.

Parent Tip: Your child should be able to label a world map with the seven continents and four major oceans. He should have a basic understanding of latitude and longitude and key locations such as the equator, prime meridian and the International Date Line. Additionally, he should have knowledge of his state geography, including major regions, major cities, and landforms.

Using the world map, locate the following:

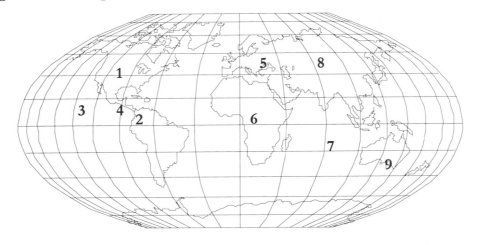

1. North America

    a. 1
    b. 2
    c. 4
    d. 7

2. Mexico

    a. 1
    b. 2
    c. 4
    d. 7

3. Europe

    a. 3
    b. 5
    c. 6
    d. 8

4. Pacific Ocean

    a. 3
    b. 5
    c. 6
    d. 9

5. Panama Canal

    a. 2
    b. 5
    c. 7
    d. 9

Using the map of California, locate

6. San Francisco

    a. 1
    b. 2
    c. 3
    d. 4

7. Monterey Bay

    a. 1
    b. 2
    c. 3
    d. 4

8. Santa Barbara

    a. 3
    b. 4
    c. 5
    d. 6

9. Los Angeles

    a. 1
    b. 2
    c. 4
    d. 5

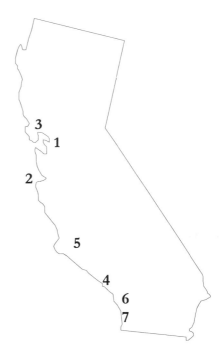

10. San Diego

    a. 3
    b. 4
    c. 6
    d. 7

11. Capistrano

    a. 2
    b. 5
    c. 6
    d. 7

12. Sacramento

    a. 1
    b. 3
    c. 5
    d. 7

SOCIAL STUDIES
Answer Key

**Physical &
Geographic
Features**

1. b
2. c
3. b
4. a
5. c
6. d
7. a
8. c
9. d
10. d
11. b
12. c
13. c
14. c
15. d

**Social,
Political,
Cultural, &
Economic...**

1. c
2. a
3. c
4. b
5. d
6. a
7. b
8. c
9. c
10. b
11. b
12. c
13. c
14. b
15. a
16. d
17. d

18. b
19. d
20. a
21. b
22. b
23. c
24. a
25. c
26. c
27. b
28. d

**Economic,
Social, &
Political Life of
California**

1. b
2. c
3. b
4. d
5. d
6. b
7. d
8. d
9. a
10. d
11. a
12. c
13. d
14. b
15. a
16. b
17. d
18. c
19. c
20. d
21. c
22. b
23. c
24. d
25. b

26. c
27. d
28. b
29. c
30. d
31. c
32. a
33. c

**California's
Economic
Development...**

1. c
2. a
3. d
4. b
5. a
6. b
7. b
8. c
9. b
10. c
11. d
12. b
13. c
14. c
15. b
16. d
17. d
18. a
19. b
20. b
21. c
22. b
23. b
24. a
25. c
26. b
27. b
28. d
29. c

30. b
31. d
32. c
33. d
34. d
35. d
36. d
37. d
38. c
39. b
40. c
41. d
42. a
43. d

**The Structure,
Function, &
Powers...**

1. a
2. c
3. b
4. a
5. d
6. c
7. a
8. b
9. a
10. b
11. d
12. b
13. a
14. d
15. c

Map Skills

1. a
2. c
3. b
4. a
5. a

6. c
7. b
8. c
9. c
10. d
11. c
12. a

SCIENCE

Content Cluster: EARTH SCIENCE

Objective: To evaluate knowledge of basic geology concepts and basic earth science principles.

Parent Tip: Help your children understand that minerals are the basic building blocks of rocks. Rocks are one of the earth's most common materials. Rocks are divided into three sub-categories (igneous, metamorphic, and sedimentary). The study of rocks and common earth materials provides information about the origin of our planet and its ongoing development through time.

   Additionally, other forces of nature cause great change in the earth, both short and long term. Erosion and deposition constantly change the face of the planet during long periods of time. Volcanoes and earthquakes can cause great change in short periods of time.

Choose the best answer:

1. The basic building blocks of rocks are _____.

   a. graphite
   b. lava
   c. minerals
   d. jewelry

2. A property of a mineral is _____.

   a. smoothness
   b. hardness
   c. color
   d. All of the above.

3. _____ is the softest of all minerals.

   a. Talc
   b. Asbestos
   c. Graphite
   d. Diamond

4. Weathering is a process that _____ rocks.

    a. makes
    b. erodes
    c. melts
    d. creates

5. Water is a(n) _____ that alters rocks.

    a. actor
    b. agent
    c. mineral
    d. living thing

6. Wind and ice will change rocks through _____.

    a. chemical change
    b. seasonal change
    c. physical change
    d. heat

7. Rocks from the _____ are most often changed by wind.

    a. desert
    b. beach
    c. mountains
    d. valleys

8. In a stream, as rocks hit each other they become _____.

    a. broken
    b. larger
    c. round and smooth
    d. sharp

9. _____ is/are made from tiny bits of rock and the remains of living things.

    a. Plants
    b. Sand
    c. Soil
    d. Beaches

10. _____ rocks form as melted rocks.

    a. Sedimentary
    b. Igneous
    c. Metamorphic
    d. Seashore

11. As pieces of rock stick together and build, a(n) _____ rock is being formed.

    a. sedimentary
    b. igneous
    c. metamorphic
    d. seashore

12. Heat and pressure change rocks into _____ rocks.

    a. sedimentary
    b. igneous
    c. metamorphic
    d. seashore

13. Lava is an example of a(n) _____ rock.

    a. sedimentary
    b. igneous
    c. metamorphic
    d. seashore

14. Changes in rocks due to heating, cooling, erosion, and pressure is known as

    a. the water cycle.
    b. the rock cycle.
    c. the rubber cycle.
    d. the oxygen cycle.

15. Limestone is changed to marble through applied pressure and extreme heat. Marble is a(n) _____ rock.

    a. sedimentary
    b. igneous
    c. metamorphic
    d. seashore

16. An igneous rock can change into a sedimentary rock if

    a. the rock is buried.
    b. the rock is heated.
    c. the rock is cooled
    d. the rock is weathered.

17. Quartz, mica, and feldspar are all examples of

    a. rocks.
    b. minerals.
    c. sands.
    d. pebbles.

18. Minerals are made from molecules that form _____.

    a. lumps
    b. spheres
    c. blocks
    d. crystals

19. An example of a material that is soft is _____.

    a. marble
    b. chalk
    c. granite
    d. lead

20. Pollution is a form of _____.

    a. mineral
    b. weathering
    c. climate
    d. property

21. Obsidian is a well-known _____ rock.

    a. sedimentary
    b. igneous
    c. metamorphic
    d. mountain

22. Limestone is a well-known _____ rock.

    a.　sedimentary
    b.　igneous
    c.　metamorphic
    d.　mountain

23. Slate is a well-known _____ rock.

    a.　sedimentary
    b.　igneous
    c.　metamorphic
    d.　mountain

24. Heavy rains can cause serious _____.

    a.　erosion
    b.　deposition
    c.　slides
    d.　All of the above.

25. Scientists think that the continents may have been one super continent called _____.

    a.　Pangaea
    b.　tectonic plates
    c.　continental drift
    d.　continental plates

26. The most common cause of earthquakes is _____.

    a.　mountain movement
    b.　ocean movement
    c.　plate movement
    d.　lake movement

27. Common minerals found on the east coast of South America and the west coast of Africa support the theory of _____.

    a.　continental drift
    b.　continental rift
    c.　continental shelf
    d.　continental ridge

28. The _____ of earth's plates _____ the height of mountains.

    a. separating/decreases
    b. shifting/decreases
    c. shifting/increases
    d. drifting/decreases

29. A _____ is used to measure the strength of an earthquake.

    a. television
    b. sensorgraph
    c. seismograph
    d. Tsunami

30. The _____ fault is located in California.

    a. Buenos Aires
    b. San Andreas
    c. Seismos
    d. Continental

Content Cluster: LIFE SCIENCE

Objective: To evaluate knowledge of the interactions between plants and animals in the life cycle of the planet.

> **Parent Tip:** Help your child understand the interactions of living and non-living things on the Earth. She should be able to identify and analyze food chains and food webs, common producers and consumers, and the distinction between omnivores, carnivores, and herbivores. Additionally, she should be able to describe various ecosystems and identify the members of their communities and their relationships.

Choose the correct answer.

1. An ecosystem is made up of _____.

   a. living things
   b. nonliving things
   c. living and nonliving things
   d. plants and animals

2. Living things sharing the same space is known as a

   a. population.
   b. community.
   c. ecosystem.
   d. habitat.

3. _____ organisms are becoming reduced in number.

   a. Thriving
   b. Extinct
   c. Endangered
   d. Specialized

4. Organisms that live in the same place at the same time are an example of a

   a. population.
   b. community.
   c. ecosystem.
   d. competition.

5. An organism's _____ is where it lives.

   a. cave
   b. plant
   c. habitat
   d. space

6. A _____ is any living thing that cannot make its own food.

   a. consumer
   b. producer
   c. decomposer
   d. scavenger

7. A _____ is a living thing that can make its own food.

   a. consumer
   b. producer
   c. decomposer
   d. scavenger

8. A _____ is an animal that eats the remains of dead animals.

   a. consumer
   b. producer
   c. decomposer
   d. scavenger

9. A _____ is an organism that breaks down other things to get food.

   a. consumer
   b. producer
   c. decomposer
   d. scavenger

10. An example of a _____ is a worm.

   a. consumer
   b. producer
   c. decomposer
   d. scavenger

11. An example of a _____ is a vulture.

    a. consumer
    b. producer
    c. decomposer
    d. scavenger

12. An example of a _____ is a fern.

    a. consumer
    b. producer
    c. decomposer
    d. scavenger

13. An example of a _____ is a tucan.

    a. consumer
    b. producer
    c. decomposer
    d. scavenger

14. A diagram that shows how energy flows through an ecosystem

    a. Caption
    b. Food web
    c. Food store
    d. Story web

15. When organisms work together to help each other to survive, it is called

    a. cooperation.
    b. competition.
    c. survival.
    d. extinction.

16. When all of a species die out, it is called

    a. cooperation.
    b. competition.
    c. survival.
    d. extinction.

17. When organisms work against each other, it is called

    a. cooperation.
    b. competition.
    c. survival.
    d. extinction.

18. When organisms avoid competition they increase their chance for

    a. cooperation.
    b. competition.
    c. survival.
    d. extinction.

19. _____ is an example of cooperation.

    a. Competition
    b. Niche
    c. Symbiosis
    d. Parasite

20. Fleas on a cat are an example of a

    a. symbiotic relationship.
    b. parasitic relationship.
    c. friendly relationship.
    d. community.

21. Animals that travel in herds use _____ to increase their chances of _____.

    a. fear/survival
    b. competition/survival
    c. cooperation/survival
    d. energy/survival

22. An organism's role in an ecosystem is its

    a. title.
    b. purpose.
    c. prey.
    d. niche.

23. When a cat stalks a mouse, the cat is the _____ and the mouse is the _____.

    a. prey/predator
    b. predator/prey
    c. competitor/prey
    d. prey/competitor

24. Energy for all living things comes from the

    a. earth.
    b. moon.
    c. planets.
    d. sun.

25. As energy moves through a food chain it is

    a. used by the first consumer.
    b. passed on from one consumer to the next.
    c. saved for the last consumer.
    d. saved by producers.

26. An example of a likely food chain would be

    a. plant – rodent – cat – sun.
    b. sun – rodent – plant – cat.
    c. cat – plant – rodent – sun.
    d. sun – plant – rodent – cat.

27. An organism that eats only meat

    a. carnivore
    b. herbivore
    c. omnivore
    d. All of the above

28. An organism that eats plants and animals

    a. carnivore
    b. herbivore
    c. omnivore
    d. All of the above

29. An organism that consumes plant matter

   a. carnivore
   b. herbivore
   c. omnivore
   d. All of the above

30. The California Grizzly bear is an example of a(n)

   a. carnivore.
   b. herbivore.
   c. omnivore.
   d. All of the above

31. A butterfly is and example of a(n)

   a. carnivore.
   b. herbivore.
   c. omnivore.
   d. All of the above

32. A vulture is an example of a(n)

   a. carnivore.
   b. herbivore.
   c. omnivore.
   d. All of the above

Content Cluster: PHYSICAL SCIENCE

Objective: To evaluate knowledge of energy systems such as electricity and magnetism. To analyze electrical circuits, uses of magnetism, and other power sources.

Parent Tip: Help your children understand that electricity and magnetism are examples of the effects of electric charges. They should be familiar with the concept that the gaining or losing of electrons results in objects becoming electrically charged. Additionally, they should understand that magnets produce a "magnetic field" that creates a force. Lastly, electrical circuits are pathways that move electric current, and different materials conduct (move) electricity better than others.

Choose the correct answer.

1. The smallest parts of matter are _____.

   a. atoms
   b. molecules
   c. elements
   d. electrons

2. The negative charge on an atom is called a(n) _____.

   a. atom
   b. molecule
   c. element
   d. electron

3. As an object loses electrons, it will have a _____ charge.

   a. positive
   b. negative
   c. static
   d. constant

4. When two objects attract each other, they are likely to have _____ charges.

   a. common
   b. opposite
   c. equal
   d. static

5. When two objects repel each other, they are likely to have _____ charges.

    a. common
    b. opposite
    c. electric
    d. static

6. When there is an excess of non-moving electric charges in one place, you have _____ charges.

    a. common
    b. opposite
    c. equal
    d. static

7. A _____ is a particle of matter that carries a positive charge.

    a. electron
    b. proton
    c. protron
    d. neutron

8. _____ are pathways for electricity to move through.

    a. Conductors
    b. Resistors
    c. Transistors
    d. Circuits

9. _____ are materials that electrical charges move through easily.

    a. Conductors
    b. Resistors
    c. Transistors
    d. Circuits

10. _____ are filaments found in light bulbs.

    a. Conductors
    b. Resistors
    c. Transistors
    d. Circuits

11. Electricity is sometimes measured in _____.

    a. currents
    b. volts
    c. arcs
    d. batteries

12. Electric cells can also be called _____.

    a. currents
    b. volts
    c. arcs
    d. batteries

13. A _____ is a switch that stops an overload of current.

    a. amp
    b. volt
    c. circuit breaker
    d. conductor

14. An example of a non-conductor is

    a. copper.
    b. silver.
    c. aluminum.
    d. rubber.

15. An example of a conductor is

    a. aluminum.
    b. wool.
    c. cotton.
    d. rubber.

16. A common light switch in the "off" position _____.

    a. has electricity flowing
    b. has a break in the circuit stopping the flow of electricity
    c. has a broken switch
    d. has an open circuit

17. A fuse will _____ to stop the flow of electricity in an overload.

    a. snap
    b. quit
    c. overload
    d. melt

18. An unsafe situation is found when there is a(n) _____.

    a. open circuit
    b. closed circuit
    c. short circuit
    d. long circuit

19. A magnet has _____ pole(s).

    a. one
    b. two
    c. three
    d. four

20. Magnetic poles are labeled _____ and _____.

    a. top/bottom
    b. weak/strong
    c. south/north
    d. west/east

21. When magnets pull toward each other they are said to _____.

    a. attract
    b. repel
    c. connect
    d. disperse

22. When magnets push away from each other they are said to _____.

    a. attract
    b. repel
    c. connect
    d. disperse

23. True magnetic north is located at.

    a. the northern hemisphere.
    b. the North Pole.
    c. the southern hemisphere.
    d. the South Pole.

24. A core of iron or steel wrapped in a coil of electric current is

    a. an example of current electricity.
    b. an example of a hydroelectricity.
    c. an example of an electromagnet.
    d. an example of a short circuit.

25. The term AC stands for

    a. active current.
    b. ancient current.
    c. always current.
    d. alternating current.

26. The term DC stands for

    a. designated current.
    b. direct current.
    c. dispersed current.
    d. determined current.

27. A D-cell battery uses _____ energy to produce electricity.

    a. chemical
    b. physical
    c. recycled
    d. constant

28. Electrical currents that flow in only one direction are examples of

    a. alternating currents.
    b. inconsistent currents.
    c. consistent currents.
    d. direct currents.

29. Diagram "A" shows an example of a

Diagram A

a. parallel circuit.
b. cereal circuit.
c. series circuit.
d. breaker circuit.

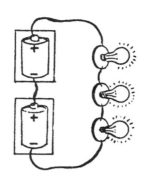

30. In diagram "A" what will happen when you remove a bulb?

a. All three bulbs will remain lit.
b. The two remaining bulbs will remain lit.
c. The two remaining bulbs will go out.
d. All bulbs are burned out.

31. Diagram "B" shows an example of a

Diagram B

a. parallel circuit.
b. cereal circuit.
c. series circuit.
d. breaker circuit.

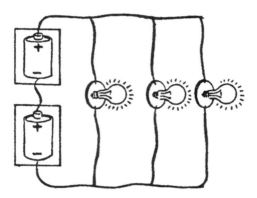

32. In diagram "B" what will happen if you remove a bulb?

a. All three bulbs will remain lit.
b. The two remaining bulbs will remain lit.
c. The two remaining bulbs will go out.
d. All bulbs are burned out.

33. Compare diagrams "A" with "B." In which situation will the bulbs glow more brightly?

a. diagram "A"
b. diagram "B"
c. both will be the same
d. all of the above

34. In diagram "C," which bulb(s) will light when the switch is closed?

Diagram C

a. A
b. B
c. Both A and B
d. Neither A nor B

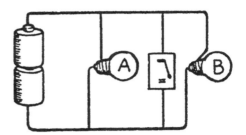

35. In diagram "D," which bulb(s) will light when the switch is closed?

Diagram D

a. A
b. B
c. Both A and B
d. Neither A nor B

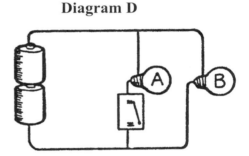

36. In diagram "E," which bulb(s) will light when the switch is closed?

Diagram E

a. A
b. B
c. Both A and B
d. Neither A nor B

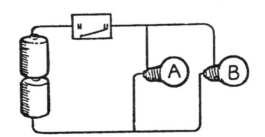

SCIENCE
Answer Key

Earth Science		Life Science		Physical Science	
1.	c	1.	c	1.	a
2.	d	2.	b	2.	d
3.	a	3.	c	3.	a
4.	b	4.	a	4.	b
5.	b	5.	c	5.	a
6.	c	6.	a	6.	d
7.	a	7.	b	7.	b
8.	c	8.	d	8.	d
9.	c	9.	c	9.	a
10.	b	10.	c	10.	b
11.	a	11.	d	11.	b
12.	c	12.	b	12.	d
13.	b	13.	a	13.	c
14.	b	14.	b	14.	d
15.	c	15.	a	15.	a
16.	d	16.	d	16.	b
17.	b	17.	b	17.	d
18.	d	18.	c	18.	c
19.	b	19.	c	19.	b
20.	b	20.	b	20.	c
21.	b	21.	c	21.	a
22.	a	22.	d	22.	b
23.	c	23.	b	23.	b
24.	d	24.	d	24.	c
25.	a	25.	b	25.	d
26.	c	26.	d	26.	b
27.	a	27.	a	27.	a
28.	c	28.	c	28.	d
29.	c	29.	b	29.	c
30.	b	30.	c	30.	c
		31.	b	31.	a
		32.	a	32.	b
				33.	b
				34.	c
				35.	c
				36.	c

MATH GLOSSARY

Acute Angle – An angle that has a measure of less than 90°.

Addend – A number that is added. In $8 + 4 = 12$, the addends are 8 and 4.

Angle – The figure formed by two rays with the same endpoint.

Area – A number indicating the size of the inside of a plane figure.

Associative property of addition – The way in which addends are grouped does not affect the sum. Also called the grouping property of addition.

    For example: $(7 + 2) + 5 = 7 + (2 + 5)$

Associative property of multiplication – The way in which factors are grouped does not affect the product. Also called the grouping property of multiplication.

    For example: $(7 \times 2) \times 5 = 7 \times (2 \times 5)$

Average – A number obtained by dividing the sum of two or more addends by the number of addends.

Cardinal number – A number, such as *three*, used to count or to tell how many.

Central angle – An angle with its vertex at the center of a circle.

Circle – A plane figure with all of its points the same distance from a given point called the *center*.

Circumference – The distance around a circle.

Common denominator – A common multiple of two or more denominators. A common denominator for 1/6 and 3/8 is 48.

Common factor – A number that is a factor of two or more numbers. A common factor of 6 and 12 is 3.

Common multiple – A number that is a multiple of two or more numbers. A common multiple of 4 and 6 is 12.

Commutative property of addition – The order in which numbers are added does not affect the sum. Also called the order property of addition.

    For example: $4 + 6 = 6 + 4$

Commutative property of multiplication – The order in which numbers are multiplied does not affect the product. Also called the order property of multiplication.

    For example: $4 \times 6 = 6 \times 4$

Cone – A space figure formed by connecting a circle to a point not in the plane of the circle.

Congruent – Having the same size and the same shape.

Cube – A prism with all congruent square faces.

Decimal – A number that is written using place value and a decimal point.

Degree (of an angle) – A unit for measuring angles.

Diagonal – In a polygon, a segment that connects one vertex to another vertex but is not a side of the polygon.

Diameter – In a circle, a segment that passes through the center and has its endpoints on the circle.

Difference – The answer to a subtraction problem. In $95 - 68 = 27$, the difference is 27.

Digit – Any of the single symbols used to write numbers. In the base-ten system, the digits are 0,1,2,3,4,5,6,7,8, and 9.

Distributive property – The general pattern of numbers of which the following is an example.   4 x (7 + 3) = (4 x 7) + (4 x 3)

Dividend – A number that is divided by another number. In 48 ÷ 6 = 8, the dividend is 48.

Divisor – A number that divides another number. In 48 ÷ 6 = 8, the divisor is 6.

Edge – In a space figure, a segment where two faces meet.

Endpoint – The point at the end of a segment or a ray.

Equal fractions – Fractions that name the same number. 1/2 and 6/12 are equal fractions.

Equation – A mathematical sentence that uses the = symbol. 14 – 7 = 7.

Equilateral triangle – A triangle with all three sides congruent.

Even number – A whole number with a factor of 2.

Expanded form – The expanded form for 5,176 is 5,000 + 100 + 70 + 6.

Face – A flat surface that is part of a polyhedron.

Factor – (1) A number to be multiplied. (2) A number that divides evenly into a given second number is a factor of that number.

Fraction – A number written in the form a/b, such as 2/3, or 11/5, or 4/1.

Greater than (>) – A relation between two numbers with the greater number given first.

Greatest common factor – The greatest number that is a factor of two or more numbers. The greatest common factor of 8 and 12 is 4.

Grouping property – See Associative property of addition and Associative property of multiplication.

Hexagon – A six-sided polygon.

Improper fraction – A fraction that names a whole number or a mixed number, such as 15/2 and 2/1.

Intersection lines – Two lines that meet at exactly one point.

Isosceles triangle – A triangle with at least two sides congruent.

Least common multiple – The smallest number that is a common multiple of two given numbers. The least common multiple of 6 and 8 is 24.

Less than (<) – A relation between two numbers with the lesser number given first.

Line of symmetry – A fold line of a figure that makes the two parts of the figure match exactly.

Lowest terms – A fraction is in lowest terms if 1 is the only number that will divide both the numerator and the denominator.

Minuend – A number from which another number is subtracted. In 95 – 68 = 27, the minuend is 95.

Mixed number – A number that has a whole number part and a fraction part, such as 3 ¼ and 6 ½.

Multiple – A multiple of a number is the product of that number and a whole number. Some multiples of 3 are 3, 6, and 9.

Multiplicand – A number that is multiplied by another number. 7 x 3 = 21. The Multiplicand is 7.

Multiplier – A number that multiplies another number. 7 x 3 = 21. The multiplier is 3.

Number pair – See Ordered pair.

Number sentence – An equation or an inequality. 3 + 5 = 8   4 < 7   9 > 6

Obtuse angle – An angle that has a measure greater than 90° and less than 180°.

Octagon – An eight-sided polygon.

Odd number – A whole number that does not have 2 as a factor.

Order property – See Commutative property of addition and Commutative property of multiplication.

Ordered pair – A number pair, such as (3, 5), in which 3 is the first number and 5 is the second number.

Ordinal number – A number, such as *third*, used to tell order or position.

Parallel lines – Lines in the same plane that do not meet.

Parallelogram – A quadrilateral with opposite sides parallel.

Pentagon – A five-sided polygon.

Percent (%) – A word indicating "hundredths" or "out of 100." 45 percent (45%) means 0.45 or 45/100.

Perimeter – The sum of the lengths of the sides of a polygon.

Perpendicular lines – Two intersecting lines that form right angles.

Place value – In a number, the value given to the place in which a digit appears. In 683, 6 is the hundreds place, 8 is in the tens place, and 3 is in the ones place.

Polygon – A plane figure made up of segments called its sides, each side intersecting two other sides, one at each of its endpoints.

Prime factor – A factor that is a prime number. The prime factors of 10 are 2 and 5.

Prime number – A whole number greater than 1 that has exactly two factors: itself and 1. 17 is a prime number.

Prism – A polyhedron with two parallel congruent faces, called *bases* and other faces are parallelograms.

Probability – A number that tells how likely it is that a certain event will happen.

Product - The answer to a multiplication problem. In 3 x 7 = 21, the product is 21.

Pyramid – The space figure formed by connecting points of a polygon to a point not in the plane of the polygon. The polygon is the base.

Quadrilateral – A four-sided polygon.

Quotient – The answer to a division problem. In 48 ÷ 6 = 8, the quotient is 8.

Radius – (1) in a circle, a segment that connects the center of the circle with a point on the circle. (2) in a circle, the distance from the center to a point on the circle.

Ratio – A pair of numbers that expresses a rate or a comparison.

Ray – Part of a line that has one endpoint and goes on and on in one direction.

Rectangle – A parallelogram with four right angles.

Rectangular prism – See Prism.

Rectangular pyramid – See Pyramid.

Regular polygon – A polygon with all sides congruent and all angles congruent.

Right angle – An angle that has a measure 90°.

Rounded number - A number expressed to the nearest 10, 100, 1,000, and so on. 352 rounded to the nearest 10 is 350.

Scalene triangle – A triangle with no two sides congruent.

Segment – Part of line, including the two endpoints.

Similar figures – Figures with the same shape but not necessarily the same size.

Sphere – A space figure with all of its points the same distance from a given point called the *center*.

Square – A rectangle with all four sides congruent.

Standard form – The standard form for 5 thousands 1 hundred 7 tens 6 ones is 5,176.

Subtrahend – A number to be subtracted from another number. In 95 – 68 = 27, the subtrahend is 68.

Sum – the answer to an addition problem. In 8 + 4 = 12, the sum is 12.

Triangle – A three-sided polygon.

Triangular prism – See Prism.

Triangular pyramid – See Pyramid.

Vertex – (1) The common endpoint of two rays that form an angle. (2) The point of intersection of two sides of a polygon. (3) The point of intersection of the edges of a polyhedron.

Volume – A number indicating the size of the inside of a space figure.

Whole number – One of the numbers 0, 1, 2, 3, 4, and so on.